Linda Bank Downs

Diego Rivera
The Detroit Industry
Murals

The Detroit Institute of Arts
in association with
W. W. Norton & Company • New York • London

Frontispiece: Rivera with sketchbook on the scaffolding in front of
the east wall central panel, 1932.

page 6: Rivera painting the south
wall figure of the yellow race,
1932.

Printed in Hong Kong
First Edition

The text and display of this book are composed in Scala Sans
Design and composition by Katy Homans
Manufacturing by South China Printing Co.

Library of Congress Cataloging-in-Publication Data

Downs, Linda Bank.
Diego Rivera : the Detroit industry murals / Linda Bank Downs.
p.   cm.
Includes bibliographical references and index.
ISBN 0-393-04529-3
1. Rivera, Diego, 1886–1957—Criticism and interpretation. 2. Mural painting
and decoration, Mexican—Michigan—Detroit—Themes, motives. 3. Mural painting and decoration—20th century—Michigan—Detroit—Themes, motives. 4. Industries in art. 5. Kahlo,
Frida. I. Title.
ND259.R5D68   1999
759.972—dc21   98-31996
                              CIP

W. W. Norton & Company, Inc., 500 Fifth Avenue, New York, N.Y. 10110
www.wwnorton.com

W. W. Norton & Company Ltd., 10 Coptic Street, London WC1A 1PU

1 2 3 4 5 6 7 8 9 0

Contents

In memory of my father, Andrew Steven Bank, and to my mother,

Margaret Wiegershaus Bank, who introduced me to the Detroit Institute of Arts

and the Diego Rivera frescoes

Just as we today study and interpret the great frescoes of Renaissance Italy and the friezes of Mayan temples to improve our understanding of the times in which those works were created, future generations will look at the powerful images in the *Detroit Industry* murals and find that they graphically reveal the values of industrial America during the first third of the twentieth century. It may seem ironic that Edsel Ford, an American industrial magnate, would commission Diego Rivera, a Mexican Marxist, to paint these enduring scenes on the museum's walls. But Rivera was the right man for the job. He brought to this task a vision encompassing much more than the simple documentation of factory processes. His images speak to the impact the industrial age had on the notion of work itself and on the changing relationship of humanity to the natural world. The murals were painted in 1932–1933 during the Great Depression, and Rivera's sympathy for the plight of the workers is abundantly clear. During the previous generation many had migrated from a rural way of life, defined by the pace of the seasons and the rhythms of nature, to urban environments and very different livelihoods, governed by the mechanical cadence of the factory with its time clocks and assembly lines. It was a time to question whether industry and its emphasis on mass production, repetitive processes, and interchangeable parts could provide a rewarding and meaningful life of work, beyond the weekly paychecks.

Although the murals are so specific to Detroit that they are often used as a visual icon for the city, they also have a universal appeal. Rivera drew on his extensive knowledge of both European and ancient Mexican art to inform his depiction of such timeless themes as birth and death, the necessity of work, and the essential resources of the natural world. He integrated these with a startlingly accurate depiction of twentieth-century manufacturing, scientific and medical discovery, and the harsh realities of the laborers' lives on the assembly line.

It is significant that Rivera took as the theme for these complex murals the relationships among the natural, human, and mechanical elements of the manufacturing process. The central image that you see when entering Rivera Court from the west is that of an infant nourished by roots reaching into the earth but also threatened by steel plowshares. The gigantic figures on the two long walls symbolize the four races, who lie on the geological strata of the earth that supply the raw material for industry. Although the two largest panels on the north and south walls depict the manufacture of the 1932 Ford V-8, the completed car itself can barely be seen. Rivera thus avoided the pitfall of leading us through a sequence of events that culminates in a finished product. Instead, he emphasized the continuous cycles of the myriad interconnections and interactions necessary to produce a vehicle as complex as an automobile.

This book gives us an extensive behind-the-scenes look at the process Rivera used to develop the murals. It publishes for the first time many of his sketches made inside the Ford Rouge plant, as well as photographs taken there by Ford photographers for the artist's reference. Rivera's compositional sketches from several stages and his more finished presentation drawings are included, as well as the enormous cartoons for the frescoes, "lost" for decades in museum storage. Although Rivera painted the entire fresco himself, the demanding preparation required for such a large project involved the help of many assistants. Their role in the hard physical work of preparing the walls, plaster, pigments, and under drawing for painting in the durable medium of traditional true fresco is discussed in some detail.

The murals have been the object of several controversies over the years, but they remain a rich visual experience for everyone who enters the light-filled Rivera Court, a dramatic space at the very heart of the museum. These frescoes are unique to the Detroit Institute of Arts and a source of pride for the museum and the city. They have stood the test of time. The publication of this book allows us to share the murals with those who cannot come to Detroit to see them and to deepen the knowledge of our visitors, who can enjoy the privilege of the direct experience of this complex work of art. Those of us who have had ample opportunity to look at the murals over the years can attest to the fact that there always seems to be something new to discover: the sparks flying off a grinding machine, the fancy braid of a horse's mane, or the detailed skyline of the city of Detroit in 1932.

I would like to thank Linda Downs, Head of Education at the National Gallery of Art, Washington, D.C., for her years of dedication in researching and analyzing every detail of the *Detroit Industry* murals. A native Detroiter, she worked for many years in the education department at the museum here. Her interest in Rivera led to the large retrospective exhibition that opened in Detroit in 1986 before its extensive national and international tour. One of the great public art works of the century, Rivera's murals repay every moment of attention that we give them.

Maurice D. Parrish
Interim Director

1. Rivera Court to the southwest,
1995.

As junior education curators at the Detroit Institute of Arts (DIA) in 1973, John B. Hunter III and I began studying Diego Rivera's *Detroit Industry* murals to write docent texts. We did not anticipate then what is to me still an astounding adventure. The murals, which form a cycle of modern industry on four walls of the central court of the museum, were and continue to be the focal point of the collections and the most popular work of art in the museum. There was no information on the murals for the public. The only publication was a small booklet distributed in 1933 and updated in the 1950s, which had long since been out of print. In the course of that research, the museum registrar opened his files to show me hundreds of photographic negatives documenting the painting of the murals that had never been printed or published. They had been given to the museum by Eleanor Ford, long after Edsel B. Ford (1893–1943), her husband, died. Edsel and Eleanor were great patrons of the Detroit Institute of Arts and in 1932 Edsel funded the murals.

When the negatives were printed they revealed an almost daily record of Rivera painting. Another half of the collection of negatives had been given to the Ford Archives of the Henry Ford Museum. This collection identified the photographer as W. J. Stettler, a company photographer who had been assigned by Edsel Ford's office to document the mural process in photographs and film. All together the documentary photographs include over four hundred images.[1] The trove of negatives was the first of the many discoveries since 1973 that are detailed in this book.

In 1977 the Detroit Institute of Arts commissioned a lecture by Francis V. O'Connor, whose book on the Works Progress Administration (WPA) Mural Project of the Depression era had just been published.[2] He suggested a thematic coherence in the Rivera murals that had not been generally recognized before. The four walls on which they are painted, which Rivera divided into twenty-seven panels, could be read as part of a continuous whole, a cycle in which the images echoed each other in form and symbolic meaning.

This lecture inspired Mary Jane Jacob, the DIA's assistant curator of twentieth-century art, and me to develop a documentary exhibition on the treatment of the Ford Motor Company's Rouge plant (named for the Rouge River), in Dearborn, Michigan, by two modern artists represented in the collection, the photographer Charles Sheeler and painter Diego Rivera. The idea corresponded with the seventy-fifth anniversary of the Ford Motor Company. Ford not only funded the exhibition but assisted us by providing an engineer, Alexander Wowk, to identify the machines and processes depicted in the Rivera murals and Sheeler photographs, which had been taken in 1931. Wowk, Mary Jane, and I spent two extraordinary weeks at the Rouge, visiting almost every part of the factory and identifying what Sheeler saw in 1931 and Rivera saw in 1932, the year he arrived in Detroit and began painting. Much of the plant was unchanged—the dramatic pour at the blast furnaces and their buggies, which carried the molten metal along railroad tracks to the rolling mills; the billet mill, with its distinctive robotlike profile; Power House #1, with its furnaces, steam pipes, and turbines; the foundry; the glass factory; the bridge over Miller Road.

The 1978 documentary exhibition "The Rouge: The Image of Industry in the Art of Charles Sheeler and Diego Rivera" was a turning point in the scholarly and popular interest in the murals. A film, *The Age of Steel,* was produced by Shelby Newhouse. Many of Rivera's assistants and acquaintances were interviewed and talked about their experiences with him. Shelby found Stettler's original 1933 documentary film of Rivera painting the murals and incorporated it into the film. What we searched for but could not find at the time of this exhibition were

2 and 3. *Detroit Industry* cartoons on exhibition in the Detroit Institute of Arts special exhibition galleries in 1933.

Rivera's cartoons, full-scale drawings for the murals (after *cartone*, the Italian word for heavy paper). The documentary photographs showed that they had been exhibited in the museum's special exhibition galleries off the Great Hall at the time the murals were painted (figs. 2, 3). They looked gigantic when compared to the architectural setting of the gallery. And they were exquisite drawings. What had happened to them? Did they still exist? There was no record of them in the registrar's catalogue of the collection. However, in the files of Clyde Burroughs, the administrator and secretary to the Arts Commission, the governing board of the museum, I found a letter signed by Rivera's wife, Frida Kahlo de Rivera: "Diego received your letter asking that the drawings remain in Detroit. He is perfectly willing to have you keep them there provided you can send him copies of the large photographs of the frescoes which were made by the Ford photographer." [3]

At that time there were many storage areas in the basement and lofts of the museum where disorganized collections of art objects, as well as office furniture, light fixtures, boxes of correspondence, notes, magazines, and memorabilia could be found. Two archivists, Marilyn Ghausi and Claudia Hummel, had been hired to look systematically at everything in storage and begin creating a Museum Archives. I alerted them to the possibility of the existence of the cartoons by showing them the documentary photographs.

About six months after the Rouge exhibition closed, Marilyn believed she had found some of the cartoons in old Storage P. Claudia and I entered Storage P the next morning and immediately saw rolled drawings, covered in brown paper, that looked like sections of the east wall nudes, the *Pharmaceutics* panel, the *Manufacture of Poisonous Gas Bombs* panel, and the *Commercial Chemical Operations* panel. (For a panel-by-panel description of the murals, please see Chapter Three.) We could see small portions of exquisite draftsmanship without having room to unroll them completely. The cartoons had pinholes in the cor-

ners from putting them up on the walls of the museum court in which the murals were painted (then called the Garden Court, now Rivera Court) to see how the composition looked from below. It appeared that the drawings had not been touched since 1933.

The largest ones, of the four races figures, which make up part of the north and south walls of the fresco cycle, were not in this group of drawings and were still missing. Claudia and I continued the search. In the most distant and dimly lit corner were what looked like dusty steam pipes that stretched the entire height of the back wall. We were astonished to find that the "pipes," which measured about two feet in diameter and were over six feet high, were actually enormous sheets of rolled drawing paper, also covered in brown paper. We carefully opened the wrapping paper, and turned back a corner of one roll. Our flashlight lit what we realized was a gigantic foot, drawn in black chalk. These were the cartoons of the races.

It took an entire day for the conservators and art handlers to get all the cartoons out of Storage P. Throughout the following work day, the conservators rolled out the cartoons on the largest open floor of the North Court of the museum and began piecing the sections together. As each section of a cartoon was unrolled or brought together to form an entire image, the visitors and staff who had gathered gasped with excitement and applauded. The cartoons were overwhelming in their beauty and monumentality (figs. 4, 5). Their discovery was particularly daunting for the graphic arts curator, Ellen Sharp, and the paper conservator, Valerie Baas. Even though the cartoons were in excellent condition, their storage, care, and display posed major challenges.

The discovery of the cartoons sparked the idea for a major Rivera drawing exhibition. Taking advantage of the International Conference of Museums, which was held in the fall of 1980 in Mexico City, Ellen Sharp and I were able to talk to colleagues from around the world about caring for these gigantic drawings, and

4 and 5. *Detroit Industry* cartoons unrolled in the north court of the Detroit Institute of Arts after their rediscovery in 1979.

we were able to begin seeing collections of Rivera's drawings. We first met with Fernando Gamboa, who was then director of the Museo de Arte Moderno. The most outstanding museologist in Mexico and a contemporary of Rivera's, he had organized two major retrospectives of the artist's work, in 1949 and 1978. He graciously shared his knowledge about public and private collections of Rivera and urged us to see as many as we could during our stay.

The very first appointment took us out to Xochimilco, famous for its floating gardens, now a suburb of Mexico City. We rang the bell to La Noria, home of Dolores Olmedo Patiño. The villa's gates opened and we were transported into another world. Peacocks and an ancient breed of hairless dogs roamed free on a vast brilliant green lawn that ended at a fifteenth-century stone house built by the invading Spanish conquistadores. The reception room was filled with Rivera's work, including many icons that we had seen only in photographs. It was a private home, but the works that hung on the walls were of museum quality.[4]

Ellen and I looked at Rivera's paintings, drawings, and watercolors until Dolores Olmedo made a regal entrance. Her striking features and pale skin were set off by pitch-black hair pulled tightly back in a chignon. She wore a huge emerald necklace with extremely large stones that seemed to drip from her neck. The afternoon light caught its many facets as she greeted us. We were served mescal, made from fermented cactus juice. She laughed when my face lit up after the first sip. Her straightforward manner put us at ease and gave us the feeling that we had known her for a long time. We called Rivera "Maestro" and she called him "Diego," having been a close friend of his. Collector of the finest works by the artist, she was now a trustee of his estate. She had read the

Rouge catalogue and praised the museum for such an outstanding exhibition. We told her about the cartoons and presented the idea of the drawing exhibition. She reminded us that the centenary of Rivera's birth would occur in 1986 and told us that the Detroit Institute of Arts should organize a major retrospective exhibition in commemoration of the artist. She let us know that we were the curators to do the job and said she would give us all her support in organizing the exhibition. Emotionally, intellectually, and physically intoxicated—by her presence, the collections surrounding us, and, last but not least, by the potent mescal—we agreed to take it on. Thus began one of the most challenging and exciting projects of my professional life. Over the next five years we worked with an outstanding team of scholars who specialized in Rivera's work: the late Stanton L. Catlin, Alicia Azuela, Jorge Manrique, Xavier Moyssén, Mildred Constantine, and Larry Hurlburt, among many others.

The year before the retrospective exhibition couldn't have been more eventful. The change in presidential administration in Mexico meant that Ellen Sharp and I had to renegotiate all the originally promised loans with a new group of administrators at the Instituto Nacional de Bellas Artes. Public collections were redistributed and we had to search for their new whereabouts. We started the photography process at the Museo Frida Kahlo. Dolores Olmedo accompanied us and asked if we wanted to see some drawings in the Rivera Archives at the museum that related to the murals in Detroit. An assistant started bringing out spiral-bound notebooks and loose sheets of drawings, hundreds of them, all made in Detroit. We knew that we could not include even a fraction of them in the exhibition, and I was particularly sad that I did not have the time to study them. I realized then that the exhibition would not be the end of our involvement with the Rivera murals in Detroit. Six years later the opportunity to study this collection came in the form of a Robert Smith Research Fellowship from the National Gallery of Art.

On the next trip to Mexico, Nancy Jones, then DIA's assistant curator of education, and I distributed loan forms to museums and private lenders. We found that many of the owners would not lend unless the Mexican government agreed not to repatriate their works. After days of negotiations, we sent a letter to all the lenders from the director of the Instituto Nacional de Bellas Artes assuring them that the government would not repatriate private collections. I returned to Detroit and left Nancy to distribute the last loan forms. The next two days, September 19 and 20, 1985, Mexico experienced the worst earthquakes in modern history. We could not get through by telephone or telegraph to Nancy or any of our Mexican friends and colleagues. Day by day we found that all the people we knew had survived. The Detroit museum staff sent supplies and collected money for the Red Cross. We were certain that the exhibition could not open in Detroit within four months. But within days we received reassuring phone calls and letters from the staff of the Instituto Nacional de Bellas Artes and collectors saying that Rivera's oil paintings and drawings had not been harmed and that they were doing everything possible to meet the shipping deadline. The Mexicans performed a modern miracle. True to Dolores Olmedo's vision, and in spite of the earth's shifting tectonic plates, the exhibition "Diego Rivera: A Retrospective" opened in February 1986, with all the Detroit cartoons on view and over 340 paintings and graphics spanning his entire career, along with a special section of photographs of Mexico taken by artists who were Rivera's contemporaries. A documentary film was made by Michael Camerini in consultation with Stanton Catlin—the only film to cover all of Diego Rivera's murals. Sponsored by a generous grant from the Ford Motor Company, it drew the largest attendance of any museum exhibition up to that time in Detroit. To those who knew no more of Rivera's work than the Detroit murals, it was a revelation. The full range of expression that led to the development of his realistic mural style was on view, from his early academic training to post-impressionism and cubism, revealing his stature as one of the most important artists of the twentieth century.

Inadvertently, the exhibition dramatized the poor physical condition of Rivera Court. It was readily apparent that the murals needed cleaning and the skylight needed repair. The newly appointed director, Samuel Sachs II, encouraged the staff to take action. Under the direction of the chief conservator, Barbara Heller, a massive cleaning and renovation project began. It took two years (1987–1988) to replace the skylight, clean the murals (this work was carried out by two of Rivera's assistants in Detroit, Lucienne Bloch and Stephen Dimitroff; fig. 242), and replace the floor so that it corresponded to the original marble and Pewabic tile design of the adjacent Great Hall. Today the murals are once again safe from the elements, and the original colors of the fresco can now be seen as they were intended by the artist.

The research required for this study of the Detroit fresco cycle has led in many directions. The manufacturing and production processes of the 1932 Ford V-8 at the Ford Motor Company's Rouge complex were studied through the expertise of Alexander Wowk. Other industries, such as the Parke-Davis pharmaceutics firm, chemical companies, Detroit Edison, and the architectural firm of Albert Kahn, which designed most of the factories for Ford, were investigated. The industries were responsive to my inquiries and some, like the Ford Motor Company, were extremely generous with information. E. P. Richardson, former education secretary and assistant director of the Detroit Institute of Arts, and Rivera's assistants, friends, relatives, and collectors in the United States, Mexico, and Europe were interviewed. Research was carried out at the Ford Motor Company Archives, the Walter P. Reuther Labor History Archives, the Bertram Wolfe collection at the Hoover Archives at Stanford University, the Jean Charlot papers at the University of Hawaii, the Clifford Wight collection at the Syracuse University Library, and the Rockefeller Family Archives.

I am greatly indebted to many individuals who have assisted in the preparation of this book. My deepest thanks go to Dolores Olmedo, who graciously and generously opened the Rivera Archives in the Museo Frida Kahlo to me on several occasions and gave permission to publish Rivera's drawings in this book; and Alicia Azuela, art historian at the Instituto de Investigaciones Estéticas, Universidad Nacional Autónoma de México, with whom I have had many discussions about Rivera and who shared research from her book, *Diego Rivera en Detroit*. At the DIA, Ellen Sharp, curator of graphic arts, Valerie Baas, paper conservator, and Barbara Heller, chief conservator, provided technical assistance in conserving the cartoons and the Rivera frescoes. Edward Sullivan, professor of art history, New York University, critiqued the manuscript and made helpful suggestions. Nancy Jones, curator of education at the Detroit Institute of Arts, and Juan Coronel, in Mexico, critiqued the manuscript outline and gave much encouragement. J. Carter Brown, director emeritus, Earl A. Powell III, director, Roger Mandel, former deputy director, and Alan Shestack, deputy director of the National Gallery of Art, awarded me two Robert Smith Research Fellowships to work on this book. Ruth Perlin took on the responsibility of the Education Division at the National Gallery of Art during my fellowship leaves. Thanks also go to Barbara Moore. Dolores Slowinski organized and catalogued thousands of notecards, photographs, and articles used in writing this book. Mary Hill Beasley put all of the notecards on-line. Marta Horgan assisted with reference searches, interlibrary loans, translations, and correspondence. Lenore de Martínez provided many translations of texts and materials. The docents and Art to the Schools volunteers of the Detroit Institute of Arts have shared the public's responses to the Rivera murals with me, prompting avenues for further research. Dennis Nawrocki carried out research on Rivera and continues to send me information related to the Detroit murals. Stanton Catlin was a supportive colleague whose breadth of knowledge and firsthand experience with the Mexican muralists were invaluable to me, as they have been to countless students. He also led me to the Clifford Wight Archives at the University of Syracuse Library and critiqued the manuscript outline. Lucienne Bloch graciously shared information from her diary and correspondence and gave many interviews related to her work on the Detroit murals and her life with the Riveras in Detroit. Stephen Pope Dimitroff shared his conversations with Rivera and his knowledge of fresco technique and told me about his work on the Detroit murals. Mimi Kotner copied relevant materials from Francis W. Robinson's files. David Watson and Terry Rosett provided translations. Laurance P. Hurlburt led

6. The Detroit Institute of Arts main entrance on Woodward Avenue, about 1930.

me to the Rivera Archives in the Museo Frida Kahlo. Diane Voss's organizational abilities revitalized the manuscript. Michael Bell, former director, Midland Art Council, assisted in contacting Dow Chemical Company personnel to research the chemical operations depicted in the murals. I am grateful for Francis V. O'Connor's vision and interpretation of the murals and for his encouragement. Henry S. Feller III, Katherine and Mary Spinney, Robert Danto, and Benjamin Sweetwine corrected errors of identification in the murals. Mary Anne Martin graciously shared photographs.

I am also grateful to those individuals who invited me to give symposium papers and lectures, thereby providing an opportunity to clarify my ideas in relation to other recent scholarship. They include Otto Karl Werkmeister, professor of the History of Art, Northwestern University, organizer of a panel on Mexican muralism at the College Art Association; Guadalupe Rivera Marin (Rivera's daughter), Dr. Beatriz Bernal, director, and Enrique San Miguel, director, C. M. Diego de Covorrubias (both, Universidad Complutense, El Escorial, Spain), who organized an international summer course on Mexican muralism; Dr. Gerardo Estrada, director general, and Lic. Carlos Foyo, coordinator, Instituto Nacional de Bellas Artes, who organized an international symposium on Mexican muralism and American realism in Mexico City; Gail Invic, curator of education, San Francisco Museum of Modern Art, who organized a symposium on the influence of Mexican muralism on Chicano art on the occasion of the Gelman Collection exhibition; Marjorie Northrup, assistant director of programs, Reynolda House; and Dolores Béistegui de Robles, director, Colegio de San Ildefonso, Mexico City, who organized an international conference on Mexican muralism in Mexico City.

I am especially grateful for the enthusiasm and creativity lavished upon this complex book by Julia Henshaw, director of publications, the Detroit Institute of Arts; Katy Homans, who designed the book; and Jim Mairs, vice president at W. W. Norton. Jennifer Boik helped extensively with the organization of the manuscript. They showed enormous ingenuity in collapsing four walls and twenty-seven fresco panels into a manageable and didactic publication. And I also gratefully acknowledge Dirk Bakker, director of photography, the Detroit Institute of Arts, for his outstanding photographs and those of his expert staff, Robert Hensleigh and Marianne Letasi.

I lovingly thank Alice Downs for research carried out at the Detroit Public Library, manuscript editing, and her willingness to index this book; and Timothy Downs for many years of support. I acknowledge the patience of Justin Downs, who grew up with Rivera research projects and believes that I mark time by them. In reality nothing compares to the joy and satisfaction of being his mother and watching his own artistic development. Thanks to the loving encouragement of Richard Ermalovich, Katherine Sylvan, Pat Wand, and Joyce Raum.

The *Detroit Industry* fresco cycle was painted in nine months from July 1932 to March 1933 by the Mexican muralist Diego Rivera (1886–1957) at the peak of the artist's career and at the height of the Great Depression (fig. 7). In 1923, after ten years of revolution, the Mexican government commissioned murals as part of a revitalization program. Rivera and the other artists José Clemente Orozco and David Alfaro Siqueiros enthusiastically painted government walls, beginning a movement they thought would change the course of history. They were members of the Mexican Communist Party who identified with the working class by drawing workman's wages, forming a union, and painting accessible subjects in public places.

Rivera had completed four major Mexican murals by 1929 when the new presidential administration officially outlawed the Communist Party. In 1929 he was in the middle of painting murals at Mexico City's Palacio Nacional, the seat of government and the presidential palace. His fellow Communists expected that Rivera would discontinue his work in protest. But to their surprise and annoyance Rivera preferred to paint. Rivera was expelled from the party. When an invitation to paint in San Francisco arrived from the California sculptor Ralph Stackpole, Rivera was released from the political pressures in Mexico.

Of the four mural projects Rivera painted before he came to the United States, it is the Secretaría de Educación Pública (1923–1924) mural, in Mexico City, and the mural in the chapel at the Universidad Autónoma de Chapingo (1926–1927) that are closest in conception and style to the Detroit mural because of their integrated thematic programs and mature artistic style. The Secretaría murals cover the interior walls of two three-story courts and present images wholly indigenous to Mexico painted in a modern realist style. The chapel at Chapingo presents an integrated program of political and biological determinism by depicting the progress of the Mexican Revolution as parallel to that of biological evolution. Rivera not only integrated politics and biology in the chapel but integrated Christian religious imagery with communist symbols in one of the most visually appealing and spiritually uplifting mural projects of his career.

Rivera believed that the *Detroit Industry* murals were his finest work. Based on his love of industrial design, his intuitive knowledge of modern technology, his understanding of ancient belief systems, and his ability to synthesize through analogy, they are a modern icon of American technology. Stylistically tied to the modern movements he participated in—cubism, classical realism, futurism, and the didactic impulse of the Mexican Mural Movement, they represent Rivera's mature mural style.

What Rivera hoped to accomplish in Detroit was partially formulated a decade before in Mexico, when José Vasconcélos was appointed minister of education by President Alvaro Obregón. Vasconcélos commissioned visual artists, among them Rivera, Siqueiros, Xavier Guerrero, and Orozco, to create a new national culture.[1] Key to the program, which was supported by major government funding, was the idea of a historical continuum between modern Mexican culture and ancient Indian culture, which was presented as the true heritage of Mexicans, rather than the culture of the Europeans, who had held political power since the sixteenth century. Rivera's murals in particular had a profound influence in shaping a Mexican national cultural identity. In his Secretaría de Educación Pública murals, he celebrated indigenous cultures by portraying traditional dances, festivals, industries, and revolutionary struggle. In his murals at the Palacio Nacional, he depicted a golden age of ancient Aztec life. For the first time in Mexican history, Indians and *campesinos* could see

Introduction

7. Rivera painting the east wall, 1932.

themselves on the public walls of important buildings as contributing to the cultural and historical development of their country. Rivera's murals also had a tremendous impact on broadening the cultural perspective of the Mexican upper classes, even if this exclusive society continued to marginalize the people who created the indigenous art that was so admired.[2]

Just as the Mexican muralists had painted images that connected ancient cultures of Mexico to contemporary Indian culture, so did Rivera introduce industry and technology as the indigenous culture of Detroit. He aspired to broaden interest in industrial design and promote a greater understanding, acceptance, and celebration of the working class as well as American engineering genius. An idealist, he saw himself as an ambassador of cultural revolution. He brought the realities of the factory into the rarefied aesthetic atmosphere of the city's art museum. The Detroit murals include the concept of the continuity of indigenous American culture. The meeting of the ancient past of North and South America in the artist's eyes represented a common Pan-American culture.

There was a similarity of historical context between Mexico City of the 1920s and Detroit in the early 1930s. Detroit was racked not by revolution but by the effects of economic collapse. It had been a small manufacturing town until the 1880s, when jobs in the railroads, lumber yards, ship building, and metal foundries swelled it to a boom town with 116,000 inhabitants. With the emergence of automobile manufacturing in the first two decades of the twentieth century, the population grew from 466,000 in 1910 to 1,720,000 in 1930, with well over a million European immigrants and 125,000 African Americans coming from the south. It was a city made up of distinct neighborhoods drawn together by work and proximity but separated by income, race, religion, and national identity.[3]

Detroit's artistic culture grew rapidly with the arrival in 1924 of a new director of the Detroit Institute of Arts, William Valentiner. In 1927 a new, greatly enlarged museum building opened.[4] The museum had evolved from a curiosity cabinet called the Detroit Museum of Art on Jefferson Avenue to a professionally run and organized art museum in the city's Cultural Center on Woodward Avenue (fig. 6). Valentiner was the first professional art museum director in Detroit. He had studied the latest concepts of installation with the great German museologist Wilhelm von Bode in Berlin and had applied them in his previous position at the Metropolitan Museum of Art in New York. A sophisticated connoisseur, Valentiner taught the history of art to members of Detroit society, such as Rivera's patrons Edsel and Eleanor Ford. He established the basis of a strong collection for the museum by acquiring major works such as Brueghel's *Wedding Dance*, which was purchased the year before Rivera arrived. The new Beaux-Arts building on Woodward Avenue was to express the philosophical importance of the arts and to be a center of cultural activity, where opera would be performed in its auditorium and a broad range of cultural interest groups, from fine arts to ornithology, would meet. Valentiner's role as director of the Detroit Institute of Arts can be equated to that of Vasconcélos in Mexico, as Valentiner also cultivated an aesthetic identity for the community. For his work in Detroit, Rivera was again supported by a visionary.

Valentiner was drawn to Rivera because of a shared philosophy in the popularizing of art, providing a cultural context for it, and understanding the necessity for a relationship between art and politics. His professional career was indelibly shaped by Wilhelm von Bode at the Berlin Museum. He was Bode's assistant in 1906 and 1907 and was at his beck and call twenty-four hours a day since he lived across the street from Bode's home. During the reign of Kaiser Wilhelm II (1888–1918) there was an extraordinary development of German art and museums.

It was a time when the history of art was emerging as an academic discipline. Scholarship was generously supported by the government and private patrons. And scholars, led by Bode, were equally dedicated to scientific discovery in art as they were to the popularization of its value. Valentiner witnessed Bode's consummate skill as a politician in administrating a large staff and orchestrating support from the government and private patrons. He was later astonished at the ease with which Bode made the transition from an imperial to republican museum after World War I. These ideas were coupled with Valentiner's own notion that great art springs from the "common man."[5] Valentiner saw Rivera as a kindred spirit. While Rivera was hardly "common," he empathized with the working class, took on the persona of a Bolshevik revolutionary, painted for the masses, and promoted the value of art for social change. He had also been instrumental in creating a new cultural context for Mexico after the revolution. In his own field Valentiner was just as revolutionary and had idealistic aspirations for the Detroit Institute of Arts and for Detroit as a major cultural center. Valentiner not only saw Rivera as just the artist who could reach a broad public within terms that were familiar to them, but who could also envision and paint Detroit's larger cultural context.

8. *Out of Work One Year,*
Charles Tsaia, 1930.

In 1932, Detroit's automobile industries employed only half the number of workers at half the wages it had in 1929 (fig. 8).[6] Rivera found a severely depressed city, where half of the people were working but two-thirds of them were living at the poverty level. Workers were, for the most part, abandoned by their employers, who tried to keep their companies alive when there was no demand in the marketplace. Rivera did not invoke the grave realities of the Depression in the Detroit murals. Instead, he concentrated on the strength of its indigenous industrial culture.

Edsel Ford, son of Henry Ford (1863–1947), was the greatest industrialist alive at the time (fig. 9). He was more interested in industrial design than in his father's passion, efficient production. He set up a design studio away from his father's eyes at the Ford Motor Company's Rouge complex, where he and the company's engineers designed automobiles, some of which were custom built.[7] Edsel Ford developed a close personal relationship with Valentiner, who, in turn, cultivated Ford's interest in art. In 1932 Edsel was not only president of the Ford Motor Company but also president of the Arts Commission of the City of Detroit, and he was involved in the Industrial Design Committee of the new Museum of Modern Art in New York. When Rivera met Ford in April 1932, the artist was at the height of his international popularity. Their shared interest in American industrial design created mutual admiration.

9. Edsel B. Ford, 1931.

The subject of the Detroit murals is the history and development of technology in the region, from its ancient form in agriculture to its most modern manifestation in the automobile. However, the meaning, symbolism, form, and style of the murals are more thoroughly within the modern Mexican tradition than anything indigenous to Detroit. The subjects of the twenty-seven panels of the cycle are described in Chapter Three and interpreted in Chapter Four.

Fresco technique is described in Chapter Two in the context of Rivera's relationships with his assistants, his patron, and the museum staff—each of whom affected the intellectual content and physical reality of the murals. Painting a fresco is not a solitary creative process. It requires the discussion and development of ideas as well as the daily coordination between the artist and a group of assistants to make the plaster and lay it up on the walls, grind pigments to make paints, and enlarge and transfer the images to the walls. Rivera's thoughts on the development of the images and themes of the murals, recorded in the diaries of Lucienne Bloch, reveal how important discourse was to the artist. True fresco technique (painting on wet plaster so that the watercolor pigment becomes part of the wall when dry) was not widely known or used by modern artists. It can be one of the most durable of any artistic mediums if all parts of the procedure are properly carried out. It is also one of the most demanding, since changing temperature and humidity affect the quality of the plaster, how fast it dries, and how the colors change as they become part of the wall. While at work the artist made considerable demands on his assistants, colleagues, patron, and, mostly, himself. In his rare moments of relaxation, he was an engaging and provoking raconteur. Both sides of Rivera are revealed by the recollections and writings of his assistants and museum staff members.

The hundreds of previously unpublished preliminary sketches that were found at the Rivera Archives, Museo Frida Kahlo, in Mexico reveal how Rivera developed the images and themes of the murals and suggest interpretations of their meaning. Along with documentary photographs and cartoons, they call into question certain previous interpretations of the murals, ranging from thoughtful insights and wishful humanism to Marxist fiction and sexual fantasy.[8] While Max Kozloff, Terry Smith, and the recent work of David Craven have provided a context in which to place Rivera's work, a thorough interpretation of the fresco cycle can only be found by reconstructing the creative process itself.[9] Kozloff clarified Rivera's role in relation to economic and political relations between Mexico and the United States and attempted to identify a dialectic in the Detroit murals. Helen Delpar's study of cultural nationalism has completed Kozloff's beginnings in this area.[10] Smith discusses modernist aesthetics and industrial propaganda of the Depression era. Craven believes that Rivera departed from the mechanistic view of industry through his representation of workers as individuals.

It has thus far not proven intellectually or aesthetically satisfactory to interpret the murals on political grounds alone. In his essay for the exhibition catalogue *The Great Utopia,* organized by the Guggenheim Museum in 1992, Paul Wood characterized the scholarly attitude associated with research on the Russian avant-garde. His analysis could also apply to the study of Mexican muralists:

> On one side there has what amounts, more or less, to a myth of buried treasure: avant-garde artworks of the heroic period that have lain in attics and basements for decades being led blinking into the light of modern scholarship. For historians of this persuasion, ideology has probably counted little next to the glamour of the quest, which can range from a tomb-robbing lust for gold in its darker reaches to an honorable desire to shed light on a lost but incontrovertibly significant chapter of twentieth century art.
>
> For other historians, the ideology factor has surely played an important role. Confronted in their own productive lives, within and without the academy, by institutional orthodoxies requiring resistance, they find that the art of the most thoroughgoing of all movements of resistance holds a powerful attraction.[11]

Rivera's ideology was formed over a lifetime not just in the ideological heat of the post-revolutionary era in Mexico. His ideology was as complex as the breadth of his intellect and spirit. His knowledge of Marx, while intuitively accurate, was primarily based on café conversation. Bertram Wolfe doubted that Rivera actually read Marx. His artistic subjects showed allegiance to the workers and underclass but his social orientation was toward a highly educated and liberal, if not wealthy, elite. Rivera was able to maintain his communistic idealism because he never actually lived it. Just as strong as his communistic idealism, and equally present in his work, were his fascination with ancient religious beliefs, his own store of Catholic iconography from his childhood, and his scientific curiosity. The work of Alicia Azuela, Francis O'Connor, Dorothy McMeekin, and José Hernández Campos, among others, illuminates the Detroit murals from these perspectives.[12] Azuela explored Rivera's political reactions during the controversy that erupted over the murals when they were unveiled in 1933 (see Chapter Five for a discussion of the controversy). O'Connor was the first to identify the directional symbolism in the murals and, as mentioned earlier, to interpret the frescoes as a cycle. McMeekin contributed a scientific context. Hernandez Campos pointed to the importance of classicism. Betty Anne Brown and Barbara Braun have documented Rivera's interest in pre-Columbian art both as a collector and as an artist who incorporated ancient iconography into his murals.[13]

Since the frescoes were unveiled, they have been a major attraction for visitors to the Detroit Institute of Arts. They represent the ethos of Detroit— the factory, working class, machines, and industry. They speak to a broad audience. Factory workers see themselves reflected in the murals with sober dignity. Automobile executives see the positive aspects of their work in the precision design, the tremendous workforce, high productivity, and clean factories. The Detroit murals have served as part of a new automotive executive's orientation tour to the Detroit area. The murals also have had a certain success in recruiting Communist Party members and union members.[14] Workers see the tyranny of the assembly line system, hazardous machines, sinister-looking foremen, the long hours and short breaks, and the division of work by race and sex. For civil rights activists of the 1960s, the murals were an inspiration to organize for reforms inside and outside of the workplace. Detroit's industrial presence in the central court of the city's art museum was and is a constant reaffirmation of the work ethic and a certain toughness of spirit of its citizens.

The murals continue to maintain their historical importance for the Michigan community. They were used as a national symbol in 1994 when President Bill Clinton, Vice President Al Gore, and Secretary of the Treasury Lloyd Bentsen spoke in Detroit at a world jobs conference. While they may no longer be used to recruit new members to the Communist Party or the auto workers union, for many years they have been a feature of the Detroit Labor History Tours, and they remain the central focus of tours of the museum. The museum has taken many opportunities to celebrate them with such works as the 1991 *Ofrenda: An Offering to Diego Rivera*, a Day of the Dead installation created in Rivera Court by Juan Coronel, Diego Rivera's grandson, who is a writer, critic, and curator. The enormous cartoons, after being displayed as part of the 1986–1987 Rivera retrospective exhibition in Detroit, Philadelphia, and Mexico City, are once again in storage. They are catalogued, photographed, and carefully preserved, with the dream of one day creating a large storage area where they can be displayed flat on racks and studied and enjoyed, at least on a limited basis.

Are we drawing closer to the conditions needed by the passage of time and world events to look at the murals squarely and see them anew? As Jean Charlot has written:

> A re-estimate of Rivera may be next, as the anecdotes he so dutifully wove into his murals lose in topical value and, therefore, in interest. When looking at Lorenzetti's frescoes, few care who were the villains and who the heroes in Sienese politics five hundred years ago. Yet Lorenzetti is alive as ever. Rivera's work, as it is drained of its journalistic meaning, may acquire added stylistic meaning and dignity for generations to come.[15]

William Valentiner, director of the Detroit Institute of Arts, met Diego Rivera when Rivera was painting murals for the Pacific Stock Exchange Luncheon Club in San Francisco in 1931 (fig. 11). At that time Rivera was well known, particularly as the leader of the Mexican Mural Movement. He had completed four major mural commissions in Mexico City and Cuernavaca. After seeing the Stock Exchange mural, Valentiner was intrigued by the artist. He soon envisioned the possibility of bringing Rivera to develop a similar project in Detroit.

Rivera met Valentiner through Helen Wills Moody, the top-ranking tennis player between 1927 and 1933 at Wimbledon, who had been an art major at the University of California at Berkeley. Wills Moody had visited Detroit in 1928 for a tennis exhibition to raise funds for the California Lawn Tennis Association and had met Valentiner on a visit to the museum.[1] Valentiner accepted an invitation to visit her when he went to San Francisco in January 1931.[2] As one of Rivera's models for the Stock Exchange mural (fig. 12), she knew Rivera and his wife, Frida Kahlo (1907–1954). She invited the Riveras to a reception for Valentiner at her home. The next day a group of people, including Rivera and Valentiner, watched her play tennis.[3]

Rivera was aware of Detroit as a great industrial center. His interest in machines began early in his childhood in Guanajuato, a former silver mining town, where he enjoyed riding in locomotives with the engineers and taking apart mechanical toys. Rivera enthusiastically talked with Valentiner about the modern industrial design he had seen in California. He believed that American engineers who created manufacturing complexes, skyscrapers, and highway systems were first-class artists and that architects were turning to engineering design for inspiration. "In all the constructions of man's past—pyramids, Roman roads and aqueducts, cathedrals and palaces—there is nothing to equal these."[4]

Valentiner recalled, "It was a great wish of his to see that city [Detroit] and study its extraordinary growth. Nothing would have pleased me more than to have Rivera represented in the Detroit museum . . . for I had always hoped to have on my museum walls a series of frescoes by a painter of our time—since where could a building be found nowadays that would last as long as a museum?"[5]

Detroit's reputation for putting the world on wheels was well known in 1931. From the 1910s through World War II, the Ford Motor Company Rouge plant was the largest industrial complex in the world (fig. 10). Begun in 1910 on 1,100 acres of land just outside of Detroit in Dearborn, it became a giant automobile production and assembly plant in the 1920s. At that time, Ford almost totally controlled the source and shipping of raw materials as well as the means of production and manufacture. Raw materials such as iron ore and coal were brought in by ship from mines around the Great Lakes and transformed into automobiles through hundreds of processes: heating, molding, milling, stamping, welding, buffing, painting, and assembly. The Rouge had the newest production processes and the first single-story assembly plants in the world, designed by the Detroit architectural firm of Albert Kahn.

At the Rouge, Henry Ford had applied a simple principle that simultaneously sped up the manufacture of automobiles and all but eliminated skilled craftsmanship. The assembly line created the division of labor into its simplest component parts. It eliminated wasted movement by making the parts move while the workers stood still. Any worker could be trained to carry out a few simple functions.

Valentiner may have envisioned a mural in Detroit similar to the one in the Stock Exchange, which is dominated by an allegorical figure, the "queen of California" (based on a portrait of Helen Wills Moody), and includes vignettes

10. The Ford Motor Company Rouge plant, 1932.

of industrial scenes. He had in mind that only the two largest wall panels in the Garden Court would be painted. He did not anticipate that Rivera would ultimately fill the entire court with images of machines and technology.

> As soon as I returned to Detroit, I proposed to the Arts Commission to bring Rivera there. I felt I had to act quickly before New York and its enthusiasts for modern art . . . captured him. . . . Rivera's interest in machinery was especially fitted to portray Detroit and its industries and would therefore appeal to likely art patrons in our city. Edsel Ford generously offered to pay a sum of $10,000 for two large murals. There was only one court in the museum which had plaster walls and which could be used for such a painting.[6]

While Valentiner had convinced Edsel Ford of the importance of the Detroit mural, he found it difficult to persuade the rest of the Arts Commission, whose members included Albert Kahn; Charles T. Fisher, founder of the Fisher Body Company; and Julius H. Haass, a major donor. He wrote to Rivera asking for examples of his work that he could present in an exhibition at the museum. Rivera's chief assistant, Clifford Wight, sent a collection of watercolors and drawings. Valentiner's return letter to Wight expressed his difficulty in getting the idea off the ground.

> Please assure Mr. Rivera that I am doing all I can to get the Arts Commission here interested in his work, as nothing would give me more pleasure than to have some work done by him in town. But I must confess that

from conversations which I have had with several of the most influential people in town, I find that the difficulties are great in this respect, partly on account of the entire lack of understanding of modern art, and partly for political reasons. I am sorry about the attitude some people take, and I am trying to do all I can to overcome this position; but how much I shall succeed I am not yet certain.[7]

From February 17 through March 16, 1931, the museum displayed Rivera's watercolors and drawings. Valentiner enlisted E. P. Richardson, assistant director and curator of education, to help him promote Rivera in the *Bulletin of the Detroit Institute of Arts:*

12. *Nude with Arms Outstretched over Head*, 1931, pencil on paper, 81.5 x 47.3 cm. The tennis champion Helen Wills Moody was the model for this study by Diego Rivera for the ceiling of San Francisco's Pacific Stock Exchange Luncheon Club fresco.

> Diego Rivera, a leader of the now famous independent school of Mexican artists which has sprung up since the Revolution, is represented in the Detroit Institute of Arts by a number of drawings and watercolors and by a loan exhibit of drawings and paintings now being held. Rivera is a type of the intellectual side of the revolution in Mexico. . . . It is interesting to find this narrative and decorative art at a time when most good painting is introspective, detached. His work is full of a strong social sense when most art is abstract. It is architectural fresco when most paintings are easel pictures. His style, distinct from that of any living artist, is an instrument of great sophistication and great simplicity which he uses to express his ideas of the world we live in. [8]

The exhibition was a public success and helped speed along the mural project. On April 27, 1931, Valentiner wrote to Rivera, "They [the arts commissioners] would be pleased if you could find something out of the history of Detroit, or some motif suggesting the development of industry in this town; but at the end they decided to leave it entirely to you."[9] It is significant that Valentiner refers to "some motif suggesting the development of industry." He clearly had symbolic or allegorical images in mind for the Detroit murals, not the stark reality of factory interiors.

The Arts Commission finally approved the fresco project on May 26, 1931. The subject and the fee were settled after several letters were exchanged between the artist and the director. The Arts Commission agreed to have Rivera paint the two largest panels on the north and south walls of the Garden Court for a sum of $10,000, to be taken from the Edsel B. Ford Fund. But when Rivera received the measurements of the panels and found that there were 164.66 square yards to paint, he realized that this would amount to less than his normal fee of $100 per square yard. He therefore wrote Valentiner that he would paint only a portion of each of the two panels.[10] The subjects of the frescoes were to be determined by the artist.

After finishing three murals in San Francisco, Rivera was called back to Mexico in June 1931 to continue work on the Palacio Nacional murals. In July the art dealer Frances Flynn Paine visited Rivera in Mexico and on behalf of the Museum of Modern Art in New York proposed a one-person exhibition. Rivera completed his work at the Palacio Nacional in October. In December 1931, Rivera, Frida Kahlo, and Paine arrived in New York by ship. Rivera's retrospective exhibition was held at the Museum of Modern Art from December 23, 1931, through January 27, 1932. He was the second artist, after Henri Matisse, to be honored in this way by the new museum. His exhibition received enormous positive media response due to the appeal of his work and the efforts of Paine, who wrote the catalogue.[11]

Paine was genuinely interested in Rivera's work, but she was also carrying out a mission established by the newly incorporated Mexican Arts Association,

13. Frida Kahlo and Diego Rivera being greeted at the train in Detroit, April 21, 1932, by Dr. William Valentiner, director of the Detroit Institute of Arts, and Clifford Wight (left), Rivera's chief assistant. Wight had arrived a month earlier in Detroit to prepare for Rivera's arrival.

14. Rivera's arrival in Detroit, left to right: Ignacio L. Batiza, Mexican consul; Diego Rivera; Jean Abbott Wight (in background); Dr. William Valentiner.

Inc. This organization was formed in June 1930 to "promote friendship between the people of Mexico and the United States of America by encouraging cultural relations and the interchange of Fine and Applied Arts."[12] Wives of several major United States investors in Mexico were founding members, including Abby Aldrich Rockefeller, wife of John D. Rockefeller, and Elizabeth C. Morrow, wife of the ambassador to Mexico from the United States, who had commissioned Rivera to paint a mural at Cuernavaca in 1930. The accessibility of Rivera's art, the fact that he was the recognized leader of the Mexican Mural Movement, his engaging and eminently quotable conversation, together with the desire of the United States and Mexican governments to promote cultural exchange that in turn would help create a positive business environment (if not one of mutual economic benefit, then at least an environment that maintained a wary political peace)—all helped make Rivera a favorite in the popular press in 1931.

Meanwhile, in late 1931, workmen were preparing the walls of the Garden Court at the Detroit Institute of Arts. Lime for the plaster was slaked and aging and the walls had been furred out. By January 1932, Detroit was ready to receive Rivera. The Museum of Modern Art exhibition closed in New York at the end of January 1932 and Valentiner received several messages from Rivera indicating that he was headed for Detroit but saying that he was delayed due to illness.[13] Both Rivera and Kahlo were down with the flu. She wrote to Clifford Wight, "I have been in bed *again* with influenza and I felt very badly. . . . This climate of New York . . . My God! is simply awful for me. But . . . what can I do? I hope Detroit will be better, otherwise I commit suicide."[14] While in New York Rivera also worked on a series of lithographs and designed the costumes for the ballet *H. P. (Horse Power)*, which had its world premiere at the end of March, attended by Rivera and Kahlo. Both Rivera and Kahlo intended to paint in Detroit and asked if an apartment could be found with a separate "room with light enough where [it] could be possible to paint."[15]

Clifford Wight sent a telegram to Valentiner on March 5, 1932, saying that he was leaving New York for Detroit that day and asking for the date of the "Ford Workers Parade [sic] which Rivera says he must not miss on any account."[16] The Ford Hunger March occurred on March 7, before Rivera arrived. An estimated 3,500 to 5,000 laid-off workers, who received no compensation while out of

15. Detroit architect and Arts Commissioner Albert Kahn, Kahlo, and Rivera, in the mural project studio at the Detroit Institute of Arts, 1932.

work, marched from the Detroit city limits to the Ford Motor Company Rouge plant to demand relief. As the unarmed crowd approached the Rouge, Dearborn police threw tear gas and firemen prepared to douse them with water. The crowd retaliated by throwing stones. Then suddenly a group of police and guards rushed out of a gate of the Rouge and fired hundreds of shots into the crowd. Five workers were killed and more than twenty wounded.[17]

This was not the first massive protest held in Detroit during the Depression, but it was the first in which company guards and city police opened fire on the participants. Five days after the attack, a funeral march was held in downtown Detroit attended by an estimated sixty thousand people who sang the "Internationale." "The volume of singing could be heard all over the city. It reverberated."[18] The *Detroit Times* reported that it was the largest demonstration of a communist nature in the United States since the Sacco and Vanzetti funeral in Boston in August 1927.[19]

The March issue of the Communist Party newspaper *The Masses* accused Edsel Ford of allowing a massacre. "You, a Patron of the arts, a pillar of the Episcopal Church, stood on the bridge at the Rouge plant and saw four workers [a fifth protester who was wounded during the march died several days later] killed and over twenty wounded. You did not lift a hand to stop it, and when the Massacre—for Massacre it was—was over, your only care was for your own hireling, Bennett, who was hit on the head with a stone."[20]

Edsel Ford was nominally the president of the Ford Motor Company. But the real power at the company was still in his father's hands. As majority stockholder and through control of the Ford staff, Henry Ford had created a repressive work environment at the Rouge in his attempts to increase production through the control of workers. The Hunger March was formed not only to protest layoffs but also to point to the working conditions at Ford. The company had taken some positive community actions during the first years of the Depression, such as subsidizing the municipal government of the nearby suburb of Inkster (where many Ford employees lived) when it collapsed, giving loans to former company employees, and offering vacant land for vegetable gardens. But the events of the Hunger March focused public opinion on the negative and destructive aspects of the company. The company and Edsel Ford

16. Presentation drawing of north wall automotive panel, 1932, charcoal on paper, 45.7 x 83.8 cm.

17. Presentation drawing of south wall automotive panel, 1932, charcoal on paper, 45.7 x 83.8 cm.

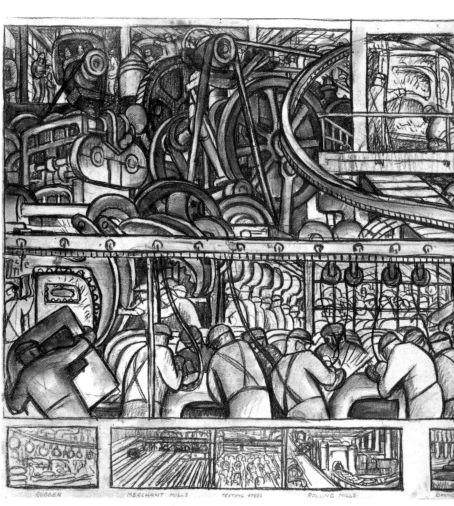

POURING INGOTS   OPEN HEARTH   SPRING TEMPERING AND CASE HARDENING   DROP FORGE UPSET FORGE   HANDFORGE   BIG FORGINGS   GLASS

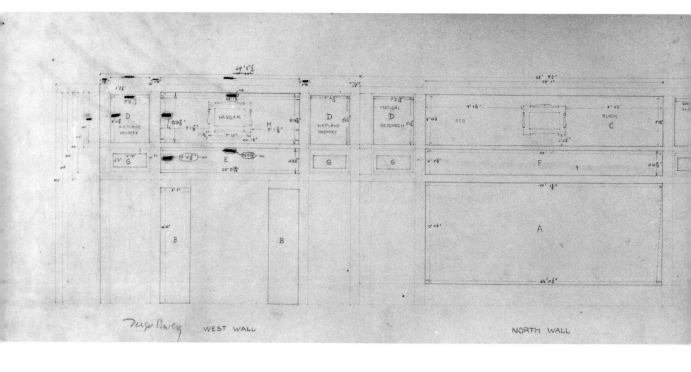

WEST WALL   NORTH WALL

18. Drawing of panels in Rivera Court with dimensions of each panel to be painted, 1932, graphite on paper.

desperately needed to rebuild a positive relationship with the public. The mural project was a convenient bridge between the Ford Motor Company and the public after this event. Ford also had major interests in Latin America and had just opened its first Mexican assembly plant in Villahermosa. Rivera was probably unaware of the magnitude of his role in respect to the company, which went far beyond the actual murals he was to paint. The company's image in Mexico would be enhanced and its public-mindedness would be demonstrated to the workers in Detroit through this commission.

Rivera arrived in Detroit on April 21, 1932, by train. He and Kahlo were met at the station by William Valentiner, Clifford Wight and his wife, Jean Abbott Wight, and Ignacio L. Batiza, the Mexican consul to Detroit, among others (figs. 13, 14). Rivera made no public statement about the Hunger March, communism, or his new patron, Edsel Ford. He spent a month studying and sketching at the Rouge and at other industrial sites. On May 21, 1932, Rivera presented the preliminary drawings (figs. 16, 17) for the north and south automotive panels to Edsel Ford and Valentiner at a dinner party arranged by one of Rivera's assistants, Lord Hastings (Francis John Clarence Westenra Plantagenet), and his wife, Lady Christina Hastings. Valentiner described the success of Rivera's designs:

> After supper we inspected the two large, precisely executed studies (about two feet by three) for the two main walls in the museum court. It was an exciting experience. Edsel Ford was carried away by the accurate rendering of machinery in motion and by the clearness of the composition, which was not confused by the great number of workmen represented, each occupied with his assigned job. The function of the machinery was so well understood that when engineers looked at the finished murals they found each part accurately designed, with one exception—Rivera had used for his model an obsolete type of machinery.[21]

After the preliminary studies were accepted by the Arts Commission the next day, May 26, 1932, Rivera began to enlarge the composition. "I was amazed at the facility he showed in constructing the skeleton: not only was the plane of the wall divided according to the golden section, which he carried in his mind—and afterwards measured for accuracy—but he also had such a clear vision of the ideal depth in which he placed his themes that this space, too, harmoniously

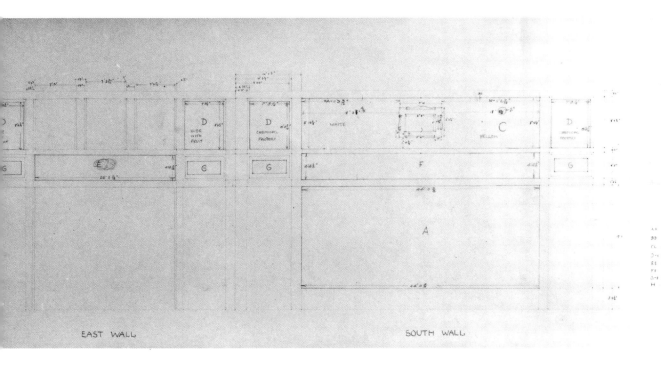

EAST WALL   SOUTH WALL

followed mathematical laws."[22] The golden section is a concept of analogous and harmonious proportion originated by the ancient Greeks and reinterpreted through the ages for use by artists and mathematicians. Rivera had learned to use it as a student at the Academia de San Carlos, Mexico City. It became second nature for him to use the golden section in both small easel paintings and in his vast mural compositions.

Edsel Ford was so enthusiastic about the plans for the murals that he promised to increase Rivera's payment from $10,000 to $20,889.[23] On May 30, 1932, Rivera returned to Valentiner with a proposal to paint all twenty-seven panels of the Garden Court (fig. 20) with the theme of the evolution of technology (fig. 18). The museum director sought Edsel Ford's approval immediately on that evening, the day before Valentiner went to Europe for an eight-month voluntary unpaid leave to help alleviate the financial problems of the museum. Even before Ford approved the new plan, Rivera was so confident about it that he asked his assistants to enlarge drawings for the additional panels. On June 10, 1932, the final contract was signed by Rivera and Clyde Burroughs, secretary of the Arts Commission. Rivera's original request for $100 per square yard was drastically reduced to an average of $27.52 per square yard when he proposed to paint twenty-seven panels (447.855 square yards) for the same amount of $20,889.[24] Rivera agreed to pay his assistants, while the museum would pay him and the cost of all materials and supplies. Rivera started to paint the frescoes on July 25, 1932, as he recorded in the fresco on the dedication paper held in Valentiner's hand on the south wall automotive panel: *These frescoes, painted between July 25, 1932, and March 13, 1933, while Dr. William Valentiner was director of the Art Institute, are the gift to the City of Detroit of Mr. Edsel B. Ford, president of the Arts Commission* (fig. 201).

THE FRESCO PROCESS

Painting a large fresco demands preparations of monumental proportions. Rivera used *buon fresco*, or true fresco, which requires painting on damp plaster with water-based pigments (fig. 19). This is one of the most durable mediums in painting, since when the pigments dry on the plaster they chemically bind and become part of the wall itself. The colors are made from natural minerals and do not fade in sunlight. Once dry, the surface is impervious to moisture and need not be coated or varnished. To make any change, the entire section of plaster must be chipped off the wall, which must be then replastered and painted. The painting of fresco can be likened to that of watercolor, where pigments can be used either transparently or opaquely, depending on the amount of water in the brush.

Rivera's use of this traditional method, which he first studied in Italy and perfected by trial and error in his early Mexican murals, required teams of contractors and assistants to prepare the walls, make the plaster, grind the pigments, and enlarge and transfer images onto the walls. Specifications for the preparation of the walls in the Garden Court and the materials needed were dictated by Rivera and sent to Valentiner five months before Rivera arrived in Detroit.[1] The specifications called for the removal of the existing plaster on the north and south walls and the construction of a grid of galvanized metal bars attached to the structural walls of the court with expansion bolts, which supported the plaster to be applied before painting (fig. 21).

Three different grades of plaster were applied in five coats. The first and coarsest grade, called the roughcast, or scratch coat, contained one and one-half parts coarse white marble dust (eighteen gauge), one part electrically roasted and thoroughly slaked lime, one part Portland cement, and long fibers (one-and-one-half-inch goat hairs soaked in lime paste; fig. 43). After this coat was applied, the surface was scratched to provide a rough tooth for the next coat and left to dry for a week. The second grade, called brown coat, consisted of two parts medium white marble dust (eighteen to sixteen gauges mixed), one part electrically roasted and thoroughly slaked lime, and short fibers (three-fourths of an inch long). This coat was smoothed out with a cork float and left to dry for a week. The brown coat, used as the surface on which the major outlines of the composition were drawn, is called the *sinopia* in Italian, referring to the red color of the paint most often used to make the drawings. These drawings are covered by the final coats of plaster. The third and final grade, called the *intonaco*, or finish coat, was made of thoroughly slaked lime and fine marble dust to create an extraordinarily smooth painting surface. The last coat was applied each day, as fresco must be painted on a fresh, damp surface (fig. 22). Sections of plaster were applied daily along major compositional divisions so that the seams could not be easily detected. Each of these sections is called a *giornata*, referring to a day's work (fig. 23). The representation of the divisions in the vast architectural spaces and elements such as the steel girders, low steel panels used as gates, and the sinuous curves of the conveyors provided useful boundaries for the edges of each section of plaster. Rivera's specifications also included designs for the construction of the scaffolding and the size (two feet by four feet) of the white marble slab for grinding colors (fig. 24).

The plaster-making center was in the museum auditorium's basement, reached at that time by a small stairway at the east end of the court (fig. 25). There were huge vats for mixing the lime and cement or sand, or the lime and marble dust, depending on which grade of plaster was in preparation. Water was added to the lime, chemically raising the mixture's temperature to the

19. Rivera painting the north wall automotive panel, 1932.

20. Garden Court, the Detroit Institute of Arts, 1931.

21. Walls being prepared for Rivera in the Garden Court, 1931. The preparation of the walls included taking down the terra-cotta reliefs, chipping off the old plaster down to the brick, and building a metal support on the two main panels, which would receive five layers of plaster. Each layer of plaster was of a progressively finer grade and thus smoother surface so that the last layer, which received the paint, was as smooth as polished marble.

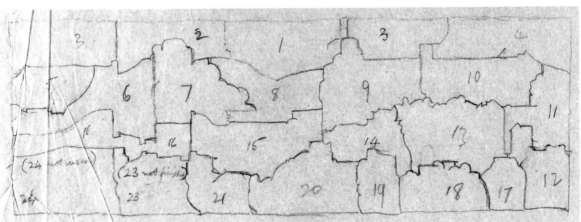

boiling point. It was then beaten with a baseball bat to get rid of any large chunks and to make it smooth. After each batch aged for weeks to let the ingredients chemically bind, it was kneaded with a garden hoe to the consistency of fine modeling clay.[2] The plaster was carried up by a pulley to the scaffolding.

Once the walls were plastered, the north and south automotive panels were divided and subdivided according to the golden section (figs. 27, 28, 29). Wight and other assistants helped Rivera with this task (fig. 26). First, a panel was divided into two equal rectangles by a center vertical line, which, for example in the north wall automotive panel, runs through the middle of the blast furnace. Diagonal lines were drawn through the rectangles from the top of the center line to the lower left and right corners. Another set of diagonal lines were then drawn from the upper left and right corners, intersecting the first two diagonals at ninety-degree angles. The points at which the second set of diagonals met the lower edge of the panel determined the golden section.

22. Rivera painting north wall automotive panel in monochrome, 1932. The wall shows two layers of plaster. The *sinopia* with the red guidelines appears below the final layer of plaster, which received the paint. The seams of the *giornate* are evident between the painted and unpainted sections.

23. Clifford Wight's drawing of numbered *giornate* of the north wall automotive panel, 1932, graphite on paper.

24. Scaffolding at the west wall, *sinopia* outlines on the panels, 1932.

25. Ernst Halberstadt preparing plaster, 1932.

26. Rivera, holding a plumb line to divide the wall for the golden section, and Clifford Wight, 1932.

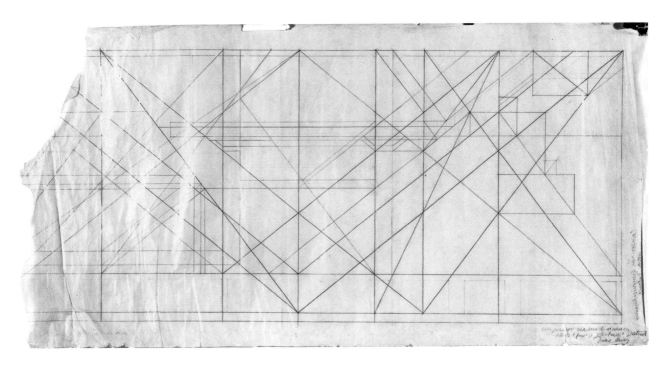

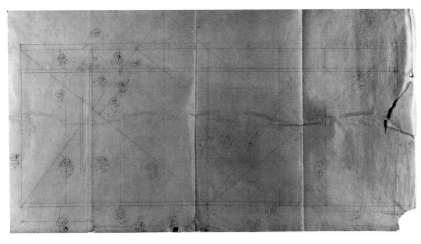

27. Drawing of the golden section for the north wall, 1932, graphite on paper, 45.7 x 83.8 cm. This drawing explores all the possibilities of dividing the north wall and where the major compositional elements could fall. The drawing could have been made before the design of the north wall automotive panel was made. However, because Rivera could divide the picture plane according to the golden section without the use of preliminary drawings, this drawing was probably done after the composition was designed in order to make minor adjustments to the composition.

28. Drawing of the golden section for north wall, 1932, graphite on paper. This drawing includes measurements of each major division of the wall according to the golden section. It was probably made to determine the placement of the *sinopia* outlines and the arrangement of the *giornate*.

Vertical lines were drawn up the wall from these points to divide the two rectangles at a ratio of approximately three to five. The giant multiple spindle on the left of the automotive panel is aligned with the golden section, as is the ladle in front of the cupola furnace, the edge of the testing room, and the center figure steadying the drill cover on the right. The four rectangles of the panel were divided again according to the golden section to create a new set of vertical lines. The compositional elements that are aligned to this second set of lines are, from left to right: the steel girders extending the length of the panel, the girders to the left of the blast furnace, the multiple spindles at the right, the crane operator's box and hook holding the drill cover, and the girders hidden by the scaffold at right.

Cartoons were created on draftsman's detail paper at the actual size of the panel. Rivera reinforced the outlines so as to see more clearly the effect of the images when the cartoons were pinned on the walls. The outlines of the images were then perforated with a small spiked wheel. The cartoons with the perforated outlines were then pinned to the panel prepared with the second grade of plaster. A muslin or cheesecloth pouch filled with two or three spoonfuls of red ocher (iron oxide), was pounced through the holes in the paper, leaving red dots on the wall. Using the dots as guidelines, outlines of the drawings were painted in red (*sinopia*) on the wall (figs. 29, 30). These then became the guidelines for plastering the final coat, which received the paint. The final coat of plaster was

29. Outline drawn in *sinopia* of the north wall automotive panel, 1932. The north wall was divided according to the golden section to assist Clifford Wight in enlarging and transferring Rivera's design.

laid up in small sections over the *sinopia* outline. Each section of the final coat of plaster corresponded to the area Rivera wanted to paint each day. The artist had about six to twelve hours, depending on the temperature and humidity, to paint on the section of wet plaster before it became too dry (figs. 31, 32, 35, 36).

Since the final coat of plaster covered the red painted outlines, new outlines were lightly scored onto it with a stylus or the butt end of a brush. The original drawings, pinned to the scaffold, reminded Rivera of the images he had designed for the section (figs. 33, 38). His assistants did not recall that Rivera made or used color sketches from which to paint. Only two small watercolors of the preliminary studies for the north wall automotive panel have been found. Ernst Halberstadt, an assistant, has pointed out: "Seeing the completed murals of this great artist it is hard to realize that these were done from pencil drawings to a symphony of colors."[3]

The paints used for fresco are, as mentioned earlier, natural mineral pigments, finely ground by hand and mixed with water (usually, distilled water) (figs. 39, 40, 41).

Distilled water is preferred for painting in fresco to insure that fungus or mold will not grow on the surface. In fact, the tap water in Detroit was so pure that it could be used, although tests were made daily.[4] The pigments Rivera used came from the United States, Mexico, and France. Some are earth colors aged for hundreds of thousands of years so that their value and hue will not change in sunlight or artificial light. Vine black (made from burned grapevine stems) came from Paris and was chosen for its translucent quality. Rivera would

start painting with vine black to create the outlines and the contours. He would then apply color over the gray and black forms. Golden ocher, used to paint the yellow race, was selected for its transparent properties to let the white of the unpainted plaster surface and the black and gray underpainting show through. The skies in the races panels are ultramarine, the brightest of blues, and French cobalt, which at that time cost twenty-two dollars a pound (most of the other pigments cost about one dollar a pound).[5] Rivera preferred painting in color in daylight.

On January 29, 1932, Valentiner wrote to Rivera in New York, "the furring out of the armature is completed and we are waiting for Mr. Wight to be here before we start with the first coat of plaster. We have arranged with our plasterer to apply the first two coats."[6] The two major north and south panels in the court were ready to be plastered. While the Riveras stayed in New York, Clifford Wight arrived in Detroit early in March to make final arrangements for the mural project.

30. Outline drawn in *sinopia* of the south wall automotive panel, 1932.

31. Rivera painting the *Manufacture of Poisonous Gas Bombs* panel with palette and brush in hand, 1932.

32. Rivera and dog on scaffolding in front of the north wall automotive panel, 1932.

33. Rivera painting the south wall *Pharmaceutics* panel with the cartoon for the panel pinned over the figure of the white race, 1933.

34. Rivera painting the north wall races panel, 1932. Rivera's brushes are visible in tin cans on the table set on the scaffolding.

35. Rivera painting the north wall automotive panel, 1932. The photograph shows the seams between the unpainted and painted sections and the final layer of unpainted plaster covering part of the *sinopia* outlines of the composition.

36. Rivera painting the north wall automotive panel, 1932. The photograph shows two layers of plaster with the *sinopia* outlines partially covered and the last layer of plaster.

37. Rivera painting the south wall automotive panel, 1933.

38. Rivera painting the south wall automotive panel with sketches pinned to the scaffold. He is watched by a group of unidentified men, 1933.

39. Frida Kahlo and Andres Sanchez Flores, 1932. Sanchez Flores adds ground pigment to water to test if it has been ground to the right consistency. Each day, dry pigment was ground on stone slabs with water. The consistency of the pigment was tested by dropping it onto water. If it sank immediately, it was not ground down enough. If it floated on the surface of the water, it was too finely ground.

40. Each color required a different amount of grinding, according to its density. A perforated cartoon on tissue paper is taped to the wall in front of Sanchez Flores.

41. Rivera's palettes, brushes, and gourds on the ledge of the court below the east wall still life, 1932. His palettes of choice were enameled white dinner plates.

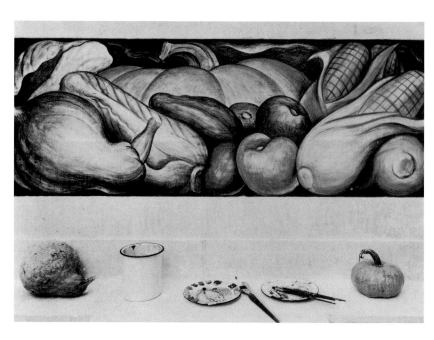

42. Detail of portrait of Valentiner on the south wall automotive panel with *sinopia* of the portrait of Edsel Ford, 1933.

43. Detail of head of a woman holding grain. Unfinished panel shows the last three layers of plaster, 1932.

44. Rivera painting the south wall *Surgery* panel, 1932.

RIVERA'S ASSISTANTS

By the time the Riveras arrived in Detroit, several of his assistants were already working at the museum: Clifford Wight, Lord Hastings, Arthur Niendorf, and Andres Hernando Sanchez Flores (fig. 47). Clifford Wight was Rivera's chief assistant in Detroit. He was originally trained as a sculptor in London, then learned the fresco technique as Rivera's assistant on the murals in San Francisco (fig. 46). Many Detroit artists had volunteered to assist Rivera with the fresco project, but Rivera relied primarily on his seasoned assistants.[7] Lord Hastings was a thirty-one-year-old mild-mannered aristocrat and artist whose mission was to support the working class, "a radical English lord and painter newly come from Tahiti, Mexico-bound to study under Rivera."[8] He first met Rivera and became his assistant in San Francisco. Valentiner's diary includes recollections of Lord Hastings and "Lady Cristina Hastings, who was Italian [Milanese] by birth, the daughter of the Italian Marchesa Cassati, well known from the fantastic red-haired portrait by Augustus John. She and Lord Hastings traveled everywhere with Rivera and reminded me of the days of the 'Grand Tour,' when the English aristocracy used to be found wherever good art was being produced."[9] He worked with Rivera in Detroit until the late fall of 1932 when the Hastingses returned to England because their visas could no longer be extended.[10]

Arthur Niendorf was "a Texan who went to Hollywood as a song writer and ended up in San Francisco working with Rivera."[11] He plastered the walls and pounced the outlines for painting. Andres Hernando Sanchez Flores, "a Mexican who worked in the sugar fields and in the Detroit automobile factories and meanwhile studied chemistry," was Rivera's chemist and prepared all of the pigments for painting.[12] He kept a log book of his chemical investigations of the pigments and the quality of the lime. The colors were first filtered to take out impurities and weighed, as the purity of the pigment was determined by weight. The colors were ground on unpolished glass with a finely polished marble adze. This was arm-wrenching, time-consuming work. Some colors, such as ultramarine, lose their intensity if ground too fine. The paints were then mixed with water and daubed onto the periphery of a white porcelain dinner plate, Rivera's palette of choice.

The other major assistants were Lucienne Bloch, painter and sculptor, who had spent ten years in Europe designing glass for a Dutch manufacturer and was the daughter of the American composer Ernst Bloch (figs. 48, 49); and Stephen Dimitroff, a twenty-two-year-old Bulgarian art student who immigrated with his family to Flint, Michigan, and studied art at the School of the Art Institute of Chicago before volunteering to work with Rivera in Detroit.[13] A young New England artist, Ernst Halberstadt described himself as a "handyman, errand boy who Wight taught to mix plaster and re-build the scaffold"[14].

Lucienne Bloch first met Rivera at a banquet given upon his arrival in New York for the opening of the Museum of Modern Art exhibition. She sat next to him and was so animated in her conversation with him that at the end of the dinner Frida Kahlo came up to her and said, "I hate you!" This was the beginning of a long and close friendship among the three of them.[15] Bloch had been on her way to Taliesin, Frank Lloyd Wright's school in Wisconsin, where she had been invited to be the head of the sculpture department. Rivera convinced her that fresco painting was much more exciting and worthwhile than working for Wright. He hired her to grind colors for the fresco panels he painted for the New York exhibition. In Detroit she lived with the Riveras in their apartment at the Wardell Hotel (now the Park Shelton apartments) next to the museum. Bloch recorded in her diary that the day after she arrived in Detroit, Rivera asked

45. Ernst Halberstadt, *Portrait of Frida Kahlo,* 1932, pencil on paper.

her to enlarge drawings. "May 30 [1932]: Started working for Diego, enlarging sketches of the huge women representing the 4 races. Lord Hastings 'was working too slowly,' said Diego. I squared the figures from 1 inch to 3 feet."[16] Many of the assistants helped enlarge drawings for Rivera by creating a grid of squares on large sheets of paper and following his designs in outlines. Rivera would then draw over them to create shading.

Stephen Dimitroff left the School of the Art Institute of Chicago with five dollars in his pocket to volunteer on the Detroit mural project. At first he gained admittance into the Garden Court by asking Rivera if he could watch him paint. Not long after, Rivera put him to work grinding pigments with Sanchez Flores. "I went upstairs and I started grinding colors. My arms almost fell off!"[17]

Studio space was adjacent to the second-floor level of the court (now the Knight Galleries). Here the drawings were enlarged to full scale. Part of this space was also used as the chemistry laboratory where Sanchez Flores weighed the pigments, ground them, and mixed them with water. Dimitroff described testing the mixed pigment until "the color stays on top of a glass of water. If any of the sediment goes down, that means that it is not ground fine enough."[18] Halberstadt saved samples in vials of all the pigments used in the Detroit frescoes and generously donated them to the DIA.

After Dimitroff had worked for a few days, Rivera asked him to pose as one of the workers in the north wall automotive panel. He was asked to take his jacket off to show his shirt. It was during the winter of 1932 and very cold in the museum. Dimitroff became ill and disappeared from the project for a few days. Halberstadt found that Dimitroff had been in bed with no food for four days. Halberstadt brought him food, then went back and told Rivera about his condition.

> He was very touched that anybody should be so dedicated that they'd do without food. Rivera paid very little, if anything, to his assistants and I don't believe [Dimitroff was] paid for a long time. And in a sense he didn't feel he had to. He probably had 10, 15, 20 letters on some days from all

46. Clifford Wight and Jean Abbott Wight in what is now the Kresge Court of the Detroit Institute of Arts, 1932.

47. Lord Hastings, Clifford Wight, Diego Rivera, and William Valentiner, 1932.

48. Lucienne Bloch with Rivera at the Rouge, 1932.

49. Lucienne Bloch (1909–1999), *Detroit: Bird's-Eye View*, 1932, lithograph, 25.8 x 35.5 cm.

50. Right to left: Rivera, Kahlo, an unidentified woman, Arthur Niendorf, and Lucienne Bloch watching an eclipse of the sun on the roof of the Detroit Institute of Arts, August 1932.

over the globe. People who wanted to come and work for nothing, just to learn how to do a fresco and be associated with him. So, in some respects it is really an honor to work for such a great craftsman.[19]

Dimitroff worked for three months before he began to be paid ten dollars a week. Halberstadt introduced him to the barter system he had been using in Detroit, trading art for food at local restaurants. Wight, Niendorf, Sanchez Flores, and Halberstadt were paid twelve dollars a week. At one point, when Halberstadt had worn holes in the soles of his shoes, he asked Rivera for a raise of six dollars a week. Rivera refused until Halberstadt threatened to make a sign reading "Rivera Unfair to Labor" and picket in front of the museum. Rivera gave him the raise but did not talk to him for a long time afterward.[20]

Halberstadt had earlier worked as an assistant to the American academic muralist Ezra Winter, who was painting in New York in 1932. Winter introduced Halberstadt to Raymond Hood, the architect of Rockefeller Center, and Hood introduced Halberstadt to Rivera in September 1932, just after the Rockefeller Center mural commission (see Chapter Five) was announced.[21] Halberstadt recalled, "Rivera . . . looked at my folio and miscellaneous other things and hired me to come to Detroit."[22] Halberstadt arrived in Detroit in late October, when winter winds begin to penetrate the city. The museum budget had been severely cut by the City Council (from $400,000 in 1928 to $40,000 in 1932).[23] Heat was scarce in the basement of the museum. Halberstadt recalled, "My

work . . . was essentially a laborer's: construction, mixing plaster. For a long
time I worked on building the scaffolding, preparing most of the plaster down
in a very cold cellar in the winter time. Very cold. There is a sketch [photograph]
of me . . . showing my sheepskin leather jacket I had to wear over two or three
woolen shirts to keep warm when working. . . . Competent craftsmanship was
accomplished in the cold of that damn cellar."[24]

Pablo Davis arrived in Detroit in the winter of 1932. He was a sixteen-year-
old boy from Philadelphia with the name of Paul Kleinbordt. He was on proba-
tion after being arrested at fourteen during a coal miners strike in Pottsville,
Pennsylvania, and served a six-month prison sentence. He was studying art in a
Philadelphia high school and saw a newspaper article showing Rivera painting
in Detroit. he was greatly enamored of the Mexican Revolution and wanted
to see Rivera paint. He saved sixty cents and hopped a freight train during
Christmas break. Once Rivera found out that Davis was a radical art student he
warmly embraced him, put him up in his apartment at the Wardell, and gave
him odd jobs to do on the mural project including touch-up painting. Rivera
was working on the upper register of the north wall at that time and asked him
to intensify the colors in order to unify the panels by painting over the dried
fresco with casein. Davis spent another short period of time in Detroit during
his Easter break in 1933. At that time Rivera was completing the south wall automotive panel. He asked Davis to paint the repair shop predella by enlarging a
small sketch Rivera had made at the Ford factory, while Rivera painted the adjacent predella of Henry Ford teaching an engineering class. Davis used the features of Dick Tracy from the comics for one of the workmen in the repair shop
to show a tough-looking worker, which pleased Rivera.[25] Rivera was not only
instrumental in kindling Davis's art interest but also his commitment to the
Communist Party. When Davis left to return to school Rivera gave him a note

51. Rivera asleep with Kahlo on
Belle Isle, an island park in the
Detroit River, 1932.

53

52. Rivera painting iron ore in the north wall middle register, 1932.

53. Frida Kahlo on the balcony of Rivera Court, 1932.

to give to Mother Bluer to ask for reinstatement into the Communist Party. Mother Bluer read the note, tore it up in anger, and enrolled Davis in a special course offered by the party on the evils of Trotskyites.

When Rivera traveled around Detroit to study the various industries, his assistants often accompanied him, enjoying a day free from the hard work at the museum (figs. 48, 51). Sanchez Flores would drive, since Rivera did not know how. They were given free access to the Rouge complex. Fred L. Black, an assistant in Edsel Ford's office, recalled that he had been put in charge of Rivera's visits to the Rouge. When Rivera and his assistants first arrived, Black arranged to have Prince Louis Ferdinand, grandson of the kaiser of Germany and godson of Alfonso, former king of Spain, who was gaining experience working at the plant, act as Rivera's interpreter. He recalled one "delightful luncheon": "It struck me as kind of a humorous situation to have Diego Rivera, labeled a communist, and who didn't believe in royalty at all, sitting at the same table and being interpreted by the kaiser's grandson."[26] The other companies Rivera and his assistants visited included the Chrysler Motor Company, Parke-Davis chemical, Michigan Alkali Plant, Detroit Edison, and the Detroit Chemical Factory.[27] W. J. Stettler, the Ford photographer, often accompanied Rivera's entourage.

Clifford Wight organized the assistants and set the work schedule according to Rivera's needs. Niendorf acted as foreman. In order for Rivera to paint during the day, the last two coats of plaster had to be laid up in the dead of night. The Detroit News announced in a headline on July 31, 1932, "Artist Rivera's Assistant Must Rise with the Milkman" and listed Wight's schedule as "2:00 a.m. breakfast; 3:00 a.m. on job to prepare plaster; 10:00 to 11:00 a.m. nap; and 12:00 returns when Rivera starts to paint."[28]

As mentioned earlier, Rivera began to paint the murals on Wednesday, July 25, 1932. He started working from the upper registers down and from the left side of each panel to the right. Each section of plaster that Rivera painted on a particular day is recorded by subject in a fragment of Clifford Wight's diary of the project. For example, on July 25, Rivera painted the "sky and one hand, Indian woman"; July 26, "Two hands"; July 27, "Head"; and July 28, "Torso." Notes of "too patchy" or "too dry" in Wight's work schedule indicate that the condition

of the final coat of plaster was not adequate to paint on and would have been chipped off the wall and replastered.

The longest session recorded stretched from Sunday, the twentieth of August, till Monday, the twenty-first, when Wight labored from 11 A.M. to 8 A.M. Rivera was having difficulty with the central west wall airplane panel. When he was not satisfied with sections he had painted, his assistants chipped them off. Wight had to stay ahead of Rivera, continually replastering and redrawing. The results were worth the twenty-one hour effort. E. P. Richardson recalled, "One of the best panels, pictorially, welding an airplane, was practically free hand. He changed that very greatly from the design which was pounced on the wall for him. . . . that's the only one[,] I think[,] in which he greatly altered it when he was just working on the wet plaster. Came out very well, too."[29] Rivera ended up painting the entire central airplane panel without stopping.[30] The panel is three times larger than any other *giornata* completed in one day. Rivera probably spent several additional hours painting and repainting. Wight's diary ends with Rivera's completion of the aviation panels; apparently he was too exhausted after that to take any more notes.

When Rivera was working with the same colors on different days, it was important for them to match perfectly. The color of newly painted fresco turns slightly lighter each day until the wall is perfectly dry. To avoid inconsistency in color, all adjacent sections are painted as close in time as possible. Once painting begins, it is risky to take a day off between adjacent sections on the same panel. This is one reason why Rivera took no time off when painting the large north and south wall automotive panels.

We know the sequence of sections for the north wall automotive panel from a diagram preserved by Clifford Wight and through the careful analysis of the Detroit Institute of Arts conservators (see fig. 23).[31] The diagram indicates that Rivera started in the center of the panel. As mentioned earlier, generally the fresco painter begins in the upper left corner of a panel and works to the right in registers so that the colors of adjacent sections match. Rivera, however, started the automotive panel with the dramatic image of the blast furnace in the upper center section of the north wall. He then painted the second section to its left. Two sections are labeled number three, which probably indicates that

54. "3:30 A.M. Xmas," 1932, at the Riveras' apartment at the Wardell Hotel. Front row left to right: Yi Sanchez (Andres Sanchez Flores), Jack (Lord Hastings), Mrs. D. R. (Frida Kahlo), consul of Nicaragua, Lady Hastings; back row left to right: (Ernst) Halberstadt, Cliff's wife (Jean Abbott Wight), Diego (Rivera), and an unidentified woman.

55 and 56. A tender moment between Rivera and Kahlo on the scaffold, 1932.

they were painted on the same day. The next sequence of sections in the second register, numbers five through twelve, follows the normal path of fresco painting from left to right. The sequence is reversed in the third and fourth registers, in which sections thirteen through sixteen and seventeen through twenty-four were painted from right to left. Notations in the last two sections, "twenty-three not finished" and "twenty-four not used," may refer to double plastering jobs Wight carried out. If Rivera did not finish section twenty before it dried, the plaster, both painted and unpainted, would have been chipped off the wall and new plaster laid up for the next day's work. If section twenty-four was not used, this may indicate that Rivera let it dry without painting it. Thus it appears that Rivera took twenty-six days to paint the north wall automotive panel.

Each night after Wight or Niendorf laid up the last coat of plaster, Sanchez Flores measured the humidity in the court. Wight would call Rivera before dawn to let him know the plaster was ready and how humid it was in the court.

Bloch, who took calls between midnight and four in the morning, recalled that Rivera liked to dawdle rather than hurrying across the street to paint. "One day I asked him why he did that. The men were worried that the plaster would dry before he came. His reply was that he 'was making difficulties' for himself . . . if he had too much time, he had a bad habit of making his work too slick! Working under pressure made him paint better. I know that was true from watching him . . . paint a section a second time. It was already too familiar for a spontaneous approach."[32]

Rivera had to compose every image of all twenty-seven panels months before he finally could begin to paint.[33] It was difficult to maintain a spontaneous approach after the same image had been sketched, refined in a final drawing, enlarged to a cartoon, redrawn and transferred to the wall. By putting pressure on himself and waiting until the last moment to paint, his approach could be as quick and direct as possible. Most of the time his dawdling consisted of reading the comics in the newspapers, sending Halberstadt out for cigars, or talking with

friends. And then he would concentrate fully on painting.[34] Occasionally this strategy failed, and the assistants were all called in to chip off painted sections and replaster.

Rivera was a steady painter. What he lacked in speed he made up with his intense concentration and vast endurance.

> For him no one can be a painter without being a worker. It is easy for any-
> one who has seen him at work on a fresco to understand that as a worker
> he functions. Twelve hours, fourteen hours a day, is nothing to him when
> he is occupied. And he is so completely absorbed when painting that time
> ceases to exist for him. Everyone in Mexico remembers the occasion when,
> after more than twenty-four hours on his scaffolding in the Chapel at
> Chapingo—painting without let up and without eating, when he attempted
> to stand up, he fell to the ground and was badly injured.[35]

> Rivera was a glutton for work. When we thought he had finished after
> 18 hours, . . . he was still going back to work, sometimes for more than
> two hours. . . . We worked on New Year's Day, 1933. When we were done
> plastering, Neindorf called Diego at 8 a.m. Frida answered that she would
> give him the message that the wall was ready. Nine o'clock came, ten,
> eleven, and noon. No Diego. Art [Neindorf] was losing his composure.
> "Diego rarely does this!" he moaned. "Something must have happened."
> . . . At 12:30 Rivera walked in with a gang of friends, Mexicans, who had
> visited him at the Wardell Hotel to wish him the felicitations of the Day.
> I thought, "Oh, gosh, don't tell me he's not going to work today . . ." It
> was painful to have to scrape off a fine plastering job. Nevertheless we did
> it. The area was ripped off, replastered, and ready for the artist the next
> morning.[36]

Frida Kahlo made sure that Rivera took breaks for lunch and dinner. She and Lucienne Bloch found a Mexican grocery store so that Rivera could eat his favorite foods. Kahlo fed not only Rivera but anyone else who watched him

57. Kahlo painting *Self-Portrait on the Borderline Between Mexico and the United States*, in the Detroit Institute of Arts mural project studio, 1932.

58. Frida Kahlo, *Self-Portrait*, 1932, graphite on paper, 62 x 47 cm.

paint. Among them was José de Jesus Alfaro, an unemployed Mexican dancer, who recalled, "Frida came in every day at about eleven-thirty. Diego looked down and then descended from the scaffold. There were Coca-Cola boxes on the floor and he and Frida would sit on them and he'd say, 'Sit down, *muchachos*, sit down.' The Mexican-style food was always delicious."[37]

LIFE IN DETROIT

In Detroit Rivera was totally absorbed in painting the fresco cycle. There were no political pressures, no problems from patrons, and his work was never interrupted. Artistically, it was a peak period for Rivera. But it was not so for Frida Kahlo (fig. 58). Her stay in Detroit was wretched, physically and emotionally, although it was a milestone in her mature work. She experienced two major losses in Detroit. After trying for many months to become pregnant, she had a miscarriage and was taken to Henry Ford Hospital for a week (fig. 59). She was slow to recuperate. Jean Abbott Wight and Lucienne Bloch stayed with her when she returned from the hospital. Bloch stopped work on the mural project, and during July and August 1932 she and Kahlo experimented with lithography at the Detroit Society for Arts and Crafts, where Rivera requested studio space for them (fig. 60). They had an enjoyable time but found that it was not their medium.[38]

In September Kahlo received word that her mother had died. She traveled with Bloch and Jean Abbott Wight by train to Mexico for the funeral. After they returned to Detroit in October, Kahlo set up an easel in temporary studio space on the third floor of the museum. There she painted some of the strongest autobiographical work of her entire career (fig. 57). Rivera greatly admired his wife's work at this time: "Frida began work on a series of masterpieces which had no

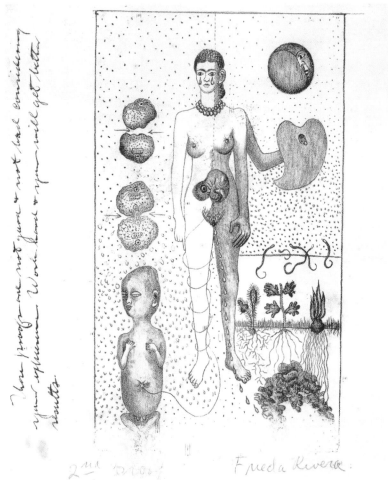

59. Frida Kahlo, *Henry Ford Hospital,* 1932, oil on sheet metal, 31.8 x 39.4 cm.

60. Frida Kahlo, *Frida and the Abortion,* Frida Kahlo, 1932, lithograph, 31.8 x 23.5 cm.

precedent in the history of art—paintings which exalted the feminine qualities of endurance, truth, reality, cruelty, and suffering. Never before had a woman put such agonized poetry on canvas as Frida did at this time in Detroit."[39] It is ironic that Kahlo's tiny paintings done in this difficult time in Detroit have now become well known and a significant part of world popular culture, and Rivera's gigantic murals covering the entire central court of the Detroit Institute of Arts, which were intended to reach the masses, are little known outside of that city.

Although the social scene diminished during the Depression, Detroiters were hospitable to Rivera, Kahlo, and the chief assistants and their wives. The Riveras, the Hastingses, and the Wights were invited to dinners, dances, and teas by Edsel and Eleanor Ford, Henry and Clara Ford, Robert H. Tannahill (an important collector), and the Albert Kahns, among others. It must have been a challenge to entertain them: the expansive Rivera speaking Spanish and French and demanding all the attention, with the petite and caustic Kahlo dressed in colorful Mexican costumes; the aristocratic Lord Hastings and his sophisticated but manic-depressive wife, Cristina; and the handsome and industrious Clifford Wight with his beautiful but dull wife, Jean Abbott Wight (fig. 46). Rivera took great pleasure in having an audience of any kind (fig. 61) and enjoyed socializing with the Grosse Pointe, Birmingham, and Dearborn elite (fig. 62). Kahlo, on the other hand, had little tolerance for social events. Lucienne Bloch's diary records incidents when Diego and Frida returned from social events and told of Frida's outrageous behavior. At Henry Ford's sister's home, Frida talked on about the wonders of communism. At a dinner at Henry Ford's she asked the anti-Semitic industrialist if he was Jewish. At a tea in Rivera's honor hosted by Clara Ford for her fellow Colony Club members, she used expressions such as "Shit on you!" as if she did not know their meaning.[40] Frida was retaliating against what she saw as the narrow snobbism of their hosts while at the same time amusing Diego.[41] The dinners at Edsel and Eleanor Ford's home were less eventful for Frida because of Rivera's great respect for his patron.

There were many meetings between Edsel Ford and Rivera. Ford frequently went to the museum to discuss the murals and the technical and economic problems of modern industry.[42] On one occasion, Ford gave Rivera a 1932 Ford four-door sedan (after Rivera had refused a deluxe Lincoln). The car proved extremely

useful when the Riveras, with Sanchez Flores as driver, rode back to Mexico City across the United States from New York in 1934. In return, the artist painted his patron's portrait (figs. 63, 64). Edsel Ford is presented as an icon of an American industrialist designer. He stands three-quarter length behind a drafting table in a design studio and is surrounded by the wall-sized chalk boards used at that time to develop automobile designs.[43] The design on the chalk board may be the 1933 Speedster that Edsel designed with Eugene Gregorie. The oil portrait also served as the model for the fresco portrait on the south wall automotive panel.

Although Rivera turned most lecture invitations down because of his work schedule and lack of fluency in English,[44] he was active in the Mexican community in Detroit. At Mexican American community gatherings he was very critical of the Mexican government for failing to institute reform and for outlawing the Communist Party. He also assisted members of the Mexican community to return to their homeland during the Depression. "Rivera has been making himself useful to his compatriots in Detroit. He has succeeded in getting the Welfare Commission here to furnish funds to send some two or three thousand Mexicans back to their country. This, of course, means in the end, a saving for the Welfare which has had to support these people."[45] Responding to complaints from jobless United States citizens and chambers of commerce that Mexicans were taking their jobs and welfare benefits, a national repatriation campaign began to send Mexicans back to Mexico. "The repatriation drive reached its peak in 1931, when more than 138,000 Mexicans returned to their homeland; by 1937, nearly 500,000 had left the United States."[46] Rivera realized that Mexican aliens such as migrant agricultural and industrial workers not only had a hard time finding work but became targets of prejudice and hatred. He arranged for thousands of Mexicans to have their train fares paid and a plot of land waiting for them when they arrived back home. In Detroit, Rivera's assistance was seen as a kind gesture among the Mexican community. But some repatriated Mexicans protested the government's actions because not only aliens but also American citizens of Mexican descent were sent back to Mexico.

On March 18, 1933, the very last day Rivera spent in Detroit, in the midst of packing his materials and anxious to get to New York, he took the time to dictate a letter to Edsel Ford on W. J. Stettler's behalf.[47] Rivera had relied heavily

62. Left to right: Clifford Wight, Jean Abbott Wight, Kahlo, Rivera, Clara Ford, wife of Henry Ford, and an unidentified figure at the Ford estate, Fairlane, Dearborn, Michigan, 1932.

63. *Sketch for the Portrait of Edsel B. Ford*, 1932, graphite on paper, 20.3 x 25.4 cm.

64. *Portrait of Edsel B. Ford*, 1932, oil on canvas, 97.8 x 125.1 cm.

on Stettler's photographs of the Rouge for the creation of the murals. As we have seen, Stettler also documented the painting of the murals in hundreds of photographs and thousands of feet of film. Toward the end of the mural project, he had been fired from his job at Ford for smoking. Smoking was strictly forbidden by Henry Ford, who sent his security police throughout the Rouge and even into the homes of Ford workers to enforce his policy. Rivera thanked Edsel Ford for his hospitality in Detroit, then asked if he would grant him the favor of reinstating Stettler at the Ford Motor Company.[48] Thanks to Rivera, Stettler had a long and distinguished career as a photographer at Ford.

Rivera left Detroit, and Wight, Bloch, Halberstadt, Dimitroff, and Sanchez Flores would go on to work with him in New York, at Rockefeller Center (see Chapter Five) and at the New Workers School. Bloch and Dimitroff later married and remained friends with Rivera and Kahlo, and Kahlo became the godmother to one of their children. Rivera had a profound influence on them as artists. Dimitroff and Bloch have created over forty murals throughout the United States and continued to paint and restore murals in the 1990s.

For Halberstadt, working with Rivera was an aesthetically "liberating" experience. Halberstadt had been taught by Ezra Winter that mural painting should be totally in support of architectural design, to appear as a monochromatic frieze as if carved out of marble in low relief.[49] Rivera broke all the rules to represent great depth, movement in and out of the picture plane, and brilliant color. Halberstadt became a supervisor of Works Progress Administration projects in Boston and Cape Cod and went on to become head of the Fresco and Mural Division in the Department of Painting at the Boston Museum of Fine Arts and was a very successful artist until his death in 1988. Niendorf also painted frescoes for the WPA. Lord Hastings had a long and distinguished career as a Marxist muralist and easel painter in London until his death in 1987. Sanchez Flores returned to Mexico with Rivera and continued as his chemist. Wight returned to making sculpture in London.

Upon entering the principal Woodward Avenue entrance of the Detroit Institute of Arts, the visitor is drawn by natural light in the distance like the light filtering through the apse in a Romanesque church (fig. 67). Crossing the marble lobby and ascending the shallow stairs into the barrel-vaulted Great Hall, which is lit with clerestory windows, you step through a ceremonial entrance reminiscent of ancient Egyptian, Greek, and Roman temples, where the initiate mounts a stairway and passes through long rectangular spaces leading into higher and more sacred ground. Rivera Court has become the sanctuary of the Detroit Institute of Arts, a "sacred" place dedicated to images of workers and technology.

It was the design of the central garden court of the Pan American Union in Washington, D.C., that in 1919 first drew the Detroit Arts commissioners to the Philadelphia architect Paul Cret for the Beaux-Arts design of the new Detroit art museum on Woodward Avenue.[1] The psychological effect of that indoor garden as a terminus of a progression of spaces that entice and impress the visitor appealed to the commissioners.[2] Designing the new Detroit museum took several years. With the arrival of William Valentiner as consultant in 1924, the ideas of Wilhelm von Bode were incorporated into the original designs. Von Bode emphasized the aesthetic significance of individual art objects and the sense of the evolution of art through a chronological sequence of gallery installations. The final Detroit museum design incorporated the installation of small galleries that encircle the central west-to-east spine of the museum represented by the monumental spaces of the entrance hall, tapestry hall, and the Pompeian Garden Court. "Cret exploited the processional spine to provide a legible division between the painting galleries on the left, and the historical collections on the right."[3]

When the new art museum opened in 1927, sunlight softly filtered through a rectangular cloth awning draped between each pair of carved and painted wooden beams in the Garden Court (fig. 68). The four white walls reflected the ambient light. Terra-cotta roundels with Etruscan motifs were mounted along the upper registers, and marble masques in antique style flanked each corner of the court. A huge stepped fountain, with fish in its pools and tropical vegetation in its planters, dominated the center of the court (fig. 20). The brick floor was laid in a pleasing herringbone design. The court served as a resting place from museum fatigue, a grand architectural space with the soft play of light, fresh smell of plants, and soothing sounds of water.

Rivera never experienced this lush garden atmosphere. By the time he arrived in Detroit, scaffolding had been erected and the walls of the court had been prepared for the murals, leaving the entire court gray with plaster dust (fig. 21). The Etruscan roundels had been taken down. The masques remained, interfering with the artist's plans for the murals, but he was unsuccessful in his attempts to get them removed. He pronounced the fountain "*horrorosa!*"[4]

Even though Rivera did not experience the Garden Court as Paul Cret intended it, the symbolic and ceremonial aspect of the architecture was not lost on him. He realized that he could not decorate only the two largest panels in the court according to Valentiner's original vision of the commission without taking its larger ceremonial and symbolic nature into consideration. He was aware that the court was the culmination of successive spaces as in a temple or a church and that the orientation of the court was toward the cardinal points of the compass.[5] And he could see that, although covered with dust and dead plants, the space could be brought back to its original function as sacred ground through his own vision of Detroit's industrial technology. To Rivera, Valentiner, and Edsel Ford, technology was Detroit's true deity, and the artist

66. South wall, detail of stamping press.

67. The Great Hall, which leads to the Rivera Court, forms part of a ceremonial progression of spaces from the Woodward Avenue entrance through the Great Hall to the court. The Rivera Court has become a "sacred" place dedicated to images of workers and technology. Photograph about 1930.

would make the Garden Court its sanctuary. Paul Cret's nineteenth-century notion of nature as refuge was transformed by Rivera's modern vision of power.

The court is oriented to east, west, north, and south, and Rivera's imagery follows the universal symbolic meaning given each direction. The east is the direction of beginnings—the rising sun, the origin and abundance of life. The west is the direction of endings—the setting sun, death and afterlife, and the last judgment. The north is the direction of the absence of light, darkness, and the interior world. The south is the direction through which the sun travels every day and represents light, the exterior world, and the surface of things. Rivera

incorporated these meanings into the murals to present his interpretation of
the dominant culture of Detroit—that of technology (fig. 66). In 1933, in the
midst of painting, he described the major theme of the murals.[6] After he completed the murals he again described the subjects and themes.[7] Rivera intended
to portray the geological, technological, and human history of Detroit. The
geological history begins with the depiction of the primordial alluvial and volcanic strata of raw materials and ends with their transformation into modern
machines and industry. The history of technology begins with one of its earliest
forms, agriculture, and ends with the manufacture of the automobile. Rivera
represented human history hierarchically with the four races in the top registers
and the workers below. He focused on the geographical origins of the races by
representing the four continents—Africa, the Americas, Asia and Europe. And he
visually quoted the history of figural representation in art from its ancient focus
on fertility to the modern form of individualized portraits. In Rivera's interpretation all three histories are inextricably linked on a cosmic scale analogous to
the Aztec universal order, which depends on ritual human sacrifice. Just as
Rivera provided the cultural context for the new revolutionary order of society
in Mexico through his murals, so he developed an ancient context for modern
industry in the form of Fordism in Detroit. Henry Ford conceived of his automobile industry as having power, breadth, and scope that went beyond the
human scale of management, labor, and machines to take on a universal life of
its own. Rivera instinctively understood this and compared it to Aztec cosmo-
logical beliefs.[8]

EAST WALL

Thematically, Diego Rivera's *Detroit Industry* fresco cycle begins on the east wall, where the origins of human life, raw materials, and technology are represented (fig. 69). In the center panel, an infant is cradled in the bulb of a plant whose roots extend into the soil, where, in the lower corners, two steel moldboard plowshares appear (fig. 73). Plowshares are used to plow under weeds and debris from the previous crop to replenish the soil with nutrients. They symbolize the first form of technology—agriculture—and relate in substance and form to the automotive technology represented on the north and south walls. Flanking the central panel are two seated female nudes representing fertility and the European and indigenous populations of North and South America. The nudes hold wheat and apples. Below these figures are two still-life panels representing the fruits and vegetables of Michigan and the Americas.

Rivera's seach for a suitable image for this panel moved to a more philosophic and iconic approach with a single central image, a development influenced by two significant events: Frida Kahlo's miscarriage on July 4, 1932, in Detroit (figs. 59, 60). Rivera made the cartoon of the infant in a plant (fig. 77) soon after October 21, 1932, when Kahlo returned to Detroit from her mother's funeral in Mexico. Kahlo's miscarriage became the subject of a series of drawings and paintings that mark the beginning of her mature art. Rivera created a healthy infant in the east wall, perhaps as a loving gesture to Frida.

Rivera referred to the infant in the plant as a "germ cell" representing life's origins and humanity's dependence on the raw materials of the earth.[9] The roots of the plant extend into an accurate representation of the geological strata of Michigan, composed of sand, salt, limestone, iron ore, and coal. According to Rivera, these raw materials are "the primordial reason for the existence of the city of Detroit."[10] Rivera imbedded the infant in the earth from which it derives nourishment. While the infant is protected in the bulb of a plant, it is also threatened by the plowshares in the same panel, implying the duality of technology as both productive and destructive.

Rivera stated that the infant on the east wall was also analogous to the Detroit Institute of Arts as "the central organism for the development of the aesthetic culture of the community."[11] By extension of this analogy, the art museum is embedded in the "primordial" aesthetic origins of the community. The artist was paying homage not only to the work of Valentiner but to the vision of the nineteenth-century founders of the museum and its current art commissioners. The image of the infant in the bulb of a plant showed their wish to create a temple of culture that would nurture the aesthetic development of the city while it, in turn, was being supported by the community. The infant is an icon of the interdependence of human life and nature. As such, it is a focal point for the viewer upon entering the court from the Great Hall. It serves the same visual and symbolic function as the traditional image of God in the apse of a church. Here the "godhead" is humanity and technology which serves as an underlying theme of the murals.

Rivera referred to the two nudes as "two colossal female figures [who] represent the growth of the vegetable life from the soil."[12] Nude figures abound in Rivera's murals beginning at Chapingo, then in San Francisco and Detroit, and continuing into his late murals in Mexico. They usually symbolize fecundity and fertility and relate in form to figures commonly found in nineteenth-century academic painting. The figures in Detroit, however, are more closely related to ancient Mexican sculpture. In the Museo Diego Rivera at Anahuacalli in Mexico City, which Rivera began building in 1942 to use as a residence and a space

69. East wall, fresco: *Woman Holding Grain*, 2.58 x 2.13 m.; *Woman Holding Fruit*, 2.58 x 2.13 m.; *Michigan Fruits and Vegetables*, .68 x 1.85 m. (both); *Infant in the Bulb of a Plant*, 1.33 x 7.96 m.

70. Sketch of figures kneeling over a plant for the east wall central panel, 1932, black chalk on paper. Rivera experimented with two other agricultural images. He reused the figure of Luther Burbank, the American plant breeder, nurseryman, and horticulturist (1848–1926), from his mural *Allegory of California*, at the Pacific Stock Exchange Luncheon Club. To the image of Burbank kneeling over a plant, Rivera added a kneeling woman and gave each of them sun hats.

The north wall *Vaccination* panel was completed on September 9, 1932, and could have inspired the design of this cartoon.

71. Sketches for the east wall panels, 1932, charcoal on paper. Preliminary sketches show that the nude female figures were part of the early design for the twenty-seven-panel project (see fig. 106). The first design is an orchard scene of flowering trees and a family of harvesters flanked by two men on tractors. This image is a version of *Still Life and Blossoming Almond Trees*, painted the previous year in Atherton, California.

to house his collection of ancient Mexican sculpture, there are several seated terra-cotta female figures from the Jalisco region collected by the artist. Dating from the seventh century A.D., they have the broad shoulders, boneless limbs, and perfectly round breasts of the female nudes on the east wall. Rivera drew upon this figural style from ancient Mesoamerica to represent all indigenous people of the Americas. The nudes' sculpted features are masklike, with an unselfconscious gaze toward the infant on the east wall central panel. Their perfectly ovoid heads are crowned with great shocks of hair. Originally both figures were painted with black hair. However, Rivera changed his mind and gave golden hair to the woman holding wheat. This change may have been an attempt to include both the indigenous and the European peoples that populate the Americas. In any event, they are iconic images of fertility holding the vegetal abundance of the Americas.

72. *Agricultural Scene*, 1932, black chalk over graphite, 1.3 x 7.9 m. The orchard scene then gave way to a second version, with a full-size cartoon of men harvesting sugar beets, radishes, and potatoes. Two workers pack vegetables into a box in the center. They are flanked by tractors on either side, which are, in turn, enclosed by images of vegetables growing in soil. The entire panel is framed by the roots of two large trees, presumably left over from the orchard design.

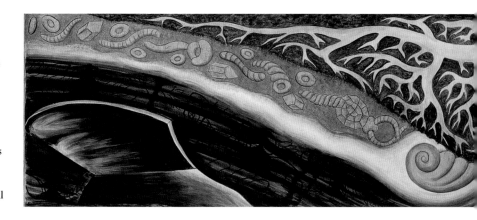

73. Detail of *Infant in the Bulb of a Plant*, fresco. The infant is cradled in a uterus-shaped plant. Below the bulb in the soil are two very large chambered nautilus shells in the stratum of salt, framing what might be a volcano and/or a vulva, from which lava and/or blood spews, nourishing the soil, which, in turn, nourishes the bulb and the infant.

74. Sketch for the east wall central panel showing two figures bending over in the lower image and the *Infant in the Bulb of a Plant* above, 1932, graphite.

75. *Infant in the Bulb of a Plant*, 1932, cartoon for the east wall, black and brown chalk over graphite, 1.33 x 7.92 m. The final image combines the agricultural theme with the nurturing theme of *Vaccination*. But instead of humans tending a child, the bulb of a plant nurtures an infant.

76. Rivera at the east wall central panel studying sugar beets. In the next to the last design for the central panel, Rivera simplified the composition even more, using a single sugar beet embedded in geological strata.

77. Rivera drawing the cartoon of *Infant in the Bulb of a Plant*, 1932.

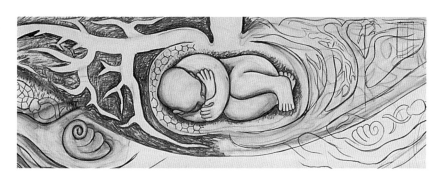

78. *Woman Holding Grain*, 1932, cartoon for the east wall, red and brown pigment with charcoal over light charcoal, 2.55 x 2.20 m. The cartoons for the female figures holding grain and apples are very similar to the final fresco images.

79. *Woman Holding Grain* and *Michigan Fruits and Vegetables*, details of the east wall, fresco. The nudes seem to be curled up to fit into the square panels on either side of the east wall. Their bulbous forms almost burst their frames. The most successful parts of the figures are the heads with their sculptural quality but with faces that are essentially expressionless. Perhaps Rivera was attempting to capture a timeless quality of expression. The heads are large in proportion to the bodies. The bodies, in turn, are diminished in size by the infant in the bulb of the plant.

Below the female nudes are two still lifes that include many fruits and vegetables. Pumpkins, squash, zucchini, corn, and several varieties of apples, plums, and peaches can be identified. They represent the abundant harvests of Michigan and the Americas. The colors and volumetric forms of these panels serve to complement the female figures above. Rivera painted these vegetables in the fall of 1932, when he began a strict diet.

Race and class were issues of Rivera's age, not gender. Rivera was admired in his time for his sexuality, while in our age he is reviled. With the rise in popularity of Frida Kahlo's image as a martyred artist, Rivera has been cast as a womanizer, misogynist, and exploiter of women. Rivera's sexual exploits were part of the male *machismo* culture of Latin America, and he could be cruelly base in his appetites. In many of his murals and society portraits, the nude female figure exudes a sexual allure which has more in common with "pin-up" pictures than high art. In Detroit the nude female figures (figs. 78, 79, 81) exude fecundity over sexual allure. They are as plump and ripe as the fruits and vegetables below them (figs. 79, 81) and are meant to represent the fertile earth of the Americas. Their gaze is introspective. Their gold and black hair reference the North and South American continents, and they reference the earth and geography. The other nude figures in the upper register of the north and south walls are explicitly about race. Here, gender subsides into androgyny. The figures exhibit masculine features, strong upper torso musculature, and frontal gazes with feminine breasts. They are gender inclusive since they represent all of humanity.

Rivera was not compelled to emphasize female sexuality in other passages of the mural where he could have capitalized on the opportunity. In the *Pharmaceutics* panel he surrounded the scientist with the legs of women who sort pills. But neither the female workers nor the scientist acknowledge their sexuality. And in the *Vaccination* panel, where Rivera used an actress as a model, he transformed the sex goddess into a protective nurse. In the representations of women, such as the upholstery workers, he presents them with the same dignity afforded the male workers, or, as with the women who are part of the tour group watching final assembly, they are caricatured for their class but not for their sexuality.

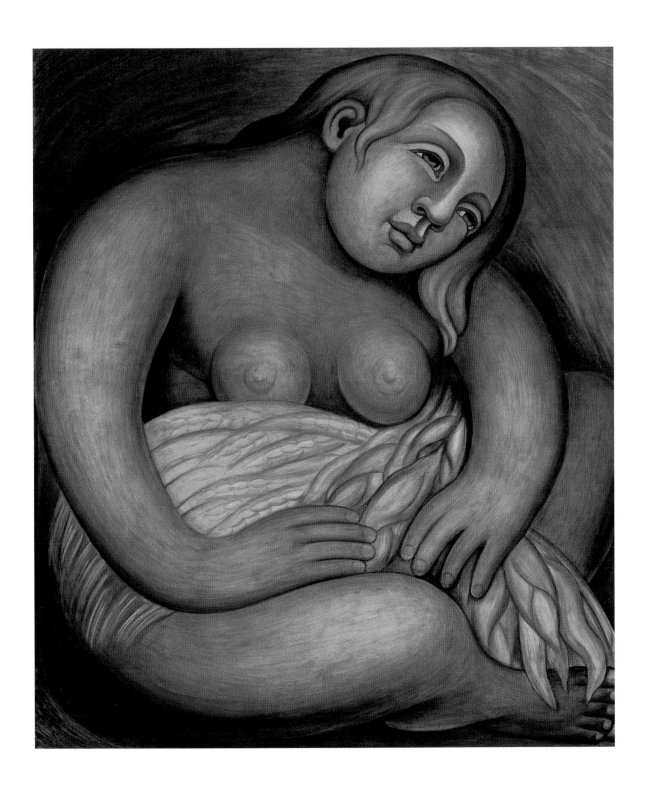

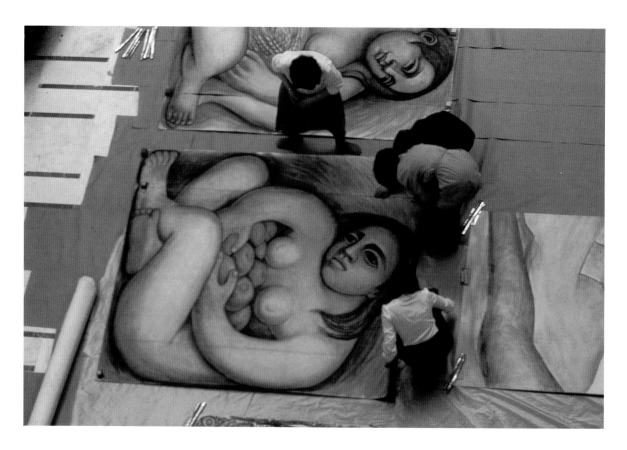

80 and 80a. *Woman Holding
Fruit*, 1932, cartoon for the
east wall, red and brown pigment with
charcoal over light charcoal, 2.55 x
2.21 m.

81. *Woman Holding Fruit*, detail
of the east wall upper panel, and
Michigan Fruits and Vegetables,
detail of the east wall, fresco.

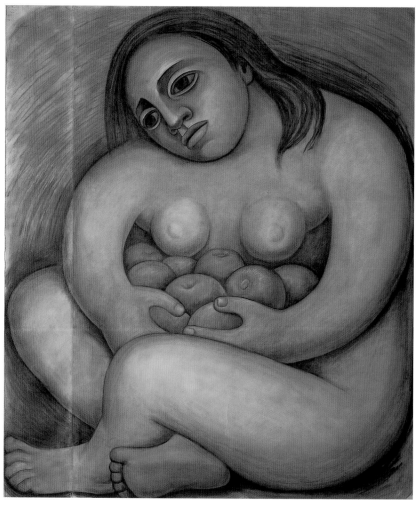

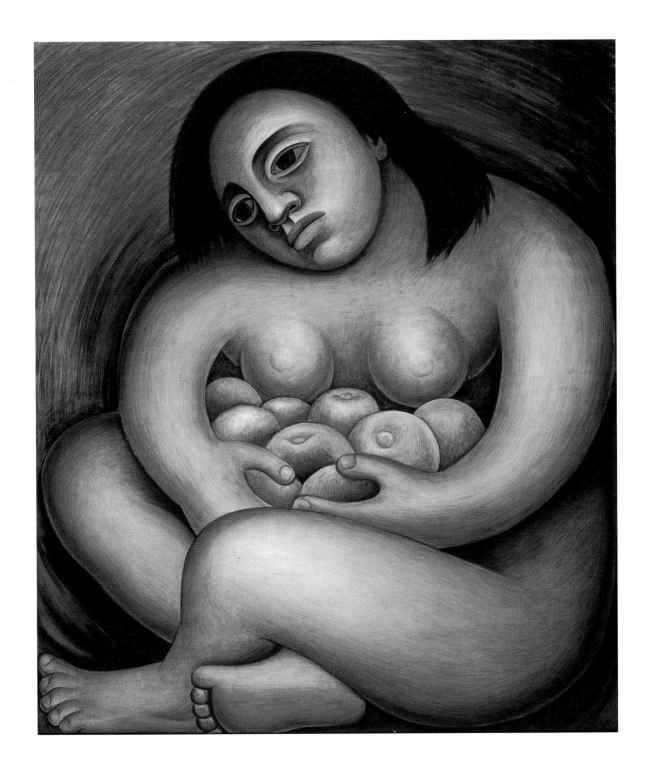

WEST WALL

The east wall theme of the development of technology continues on the west wall, where the technologies of air (the aviation industry), water (shipping and speedboats), and energy (the interior of Power House #1) are represented (fig. 82). The symbolic significance of the west wall is made explicit in the depiction of dualities in technology, nature, and humanity and in the relationship between labor and management. Rivera specifically shows the constructive and destructive uses of aviation; the existence in nature of species who eat down the food chain as well as those who prey on their own kind; the coexistence of life and death; the interdependence of North and South America; and the interdependence of management and labor. This wall combines the religious symbolism of Christian theology (the Last Judgment) with the ancient Indian belief in the coexistence and interdependence of life and death. The judgment here is related to humanity's uses of technology.

82. West wall, fresco: *Aviation*, left 2.58 x 2.13 m., center 2.58 x 7.96 m., right 2.58 x 2.13 m.; *Interdependence of North and South*, 1.33 x 7.96 m.; *The Peaceful Dove*, .68 x 1.85 m.; *The Predatory Hawk*, .68 x 1.85 m. *Steam*, 5.18 x 1.85 m.; *Electricity*, 5.18 x 1.85 m.

83. Preparation of the west wall.

84. *Aviation*, detail of the west wall, fresco. Rivera's enthusiasm for airplanes was tempered by his knowledge of their destructive uses. The airplanes on the right of the fresco are fighter planes adapted from the original designs for passenger planes. Figures in gas masks stand below. Ford sold such fighter planes to various countries around the world in the late 1920s and early 1930s. Rivera may have observed the construction of both passenger planes and fighter planes at the Stout Engineering Building, which is depicted as the hangar on the far left of this register. Rivera adjusted the perspective of the airplanes and hangar in the fresco to the vantage point of the viewer standing on the floor of the court. Not only were the architectural divisions of the upper register disregarded to extend the airplanes into the side panels, but the perspective creates the illusion of a window opening out on the hangar and airfield.

85. Ford Tri-Motor 5-AT-37 in assembly, 1929.

Upper Register: *Aviation*

In Christian directional symbolism, the west is the direction of the setting sun and the end of the world. The Last Judgment theme usually appears on the west wall of churches, depicting God saving souls in heaven on his right (the viewer's left) and damning souls to hell on his left (the viewer's right). Rivera adapted this symbolic program for a moralistic interpretation of the uses of modern technology.

In the *Aviation* panels (fig. 84), Rivera makes a clear statement about the constructive and destructive uses of technology with passenger planes on the symbolic side of the saved and war planes on the symbolic side of the damned. From 1925 through 1932, the Ford Motor Company Airplane Division manufactured planes at the Stout Engineering Building near Greenfield Village, the park of historic buildings created by Henry Ford in Dearborn. Ten days after Rivera arrived in Detroit, Ford unveiled its largest commercial transport plane, the Ford Tri-Motor, which is depicted on the left side of the *Aviation* panels (fig. 85).[13] At the same time, Ford put on a major publicity campaign for air travel. In July 1932, when Rivera began to paint the frescoes in Detroit, United Airlines, the first

86. Sketch of the west wall upper registers, 1932, graphite and black chalk on paper, 15.2 x 22.9 cm.

commercial air transport company, took over the publicity campaign from Ford. Air travel and transport captivated the public. The conquest of the air was now available to anyone who could purchase a ticket. Ford adapted the Tri-Motor for war planes and became the primary supplier during World War II.

In Rivera's view, humans mimic the constructive and destructive nature of animal life. Below the passenger planes is a dove feeding on a lower species. Below the war planes is a hawk feeding on its own species.

87. Sketch for the west wall upper and middle registers, 1932, black chalk on paper. In this early design, each plane is differentiated by subject and scale, and the architectural elements appear as separating and framing devices around the images. The upper central panel represents an airplane hangar and the two side panels depict the manufacture of fuselages and component parts. In the middle central panel a rubber tree plantation appears flanked by small panels of birds and sunflowers. The large-scale airplane panel is visually framed by the diminutive and more complicated designs in the surrounding five panels. The rubber plantation panel reinforces the symmetrical division of the airplane panel through the balanced placement of the three trees with attendant workers. This design would have been the Latin American counterpart to the North American farm scene that appears in a preliminary sketch for the east wall.

88. *The Conquest of Air*, 1932, sketch for west wall *Aviation*, pencil on tracing paper, 88.6 x 330.7 cm. This drawing breaks through the constraints of the framed architectural elements to present a longer view of the airplanes. In the center under the window frame is a skull surrounded by biomorphic forms and upturned hands with four circles in the palms. This remnant of pre-Columbian imagery was probably taken from the Mexico City sculpture of Coatlicue, the Aztec goddess of war and creation who is adorned with human hearts and skulls (fig. 185).

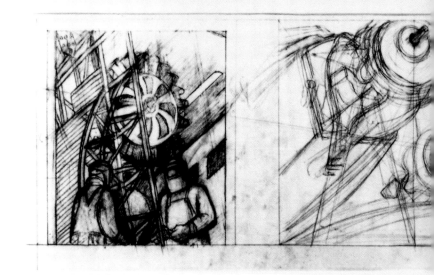

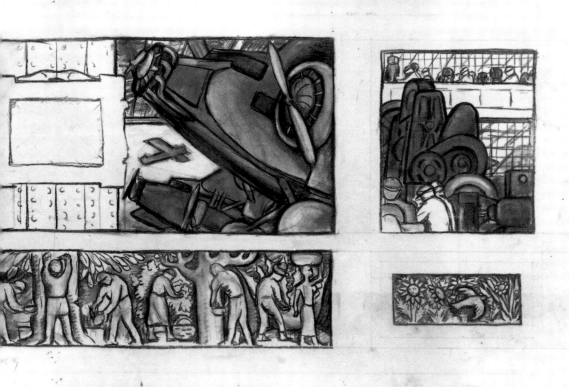

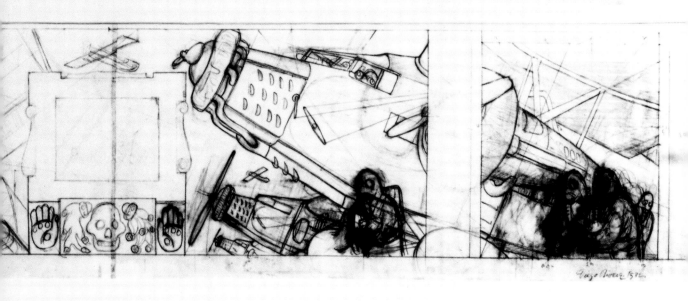

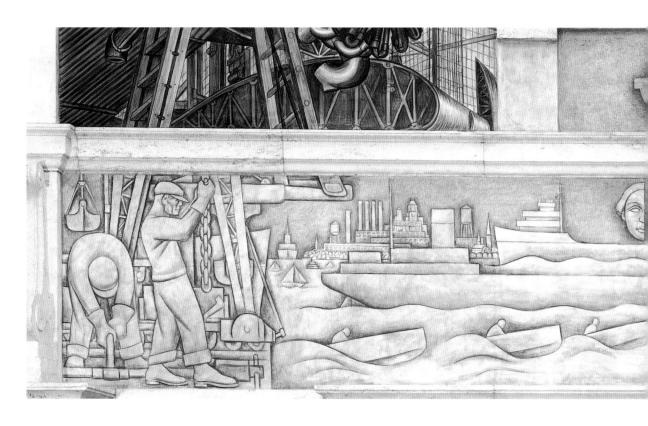

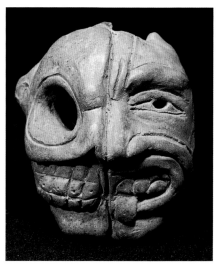

89. Life/Death mask, Tlatilco,
Mexico, 1000–500 B.C., terra-cotta.

Middle Register: *Interdependence of North and South*

While the *Aviation* panels give the illusion of windows looking out of the court onto the scene, Rivera created the opposite illusion, that of a sculpted niche, below the central window (fig. 90). Here he painted a compass rose in monochrome gray to suggest that it is carved in stone. The compass points to the northeast and southwest simultaneously. It could indicate the site of the museum, on the east side of Woodward Avenue, or it may represent the orientation of the court itself, which is slightly to the east of true north. It may allude to Rivera's own political compass, which inclined to the communism of the Soviet Union, situated far to the east of Detroit. Most likely the compass introduces the theme of the interdependence of North and South America in the middle register panel.

On the right side of *Interdependence of North and South* is a rubber tree plantation. Four men are shown collecting sap to make latex (fig. 90). In an attempt to become independent of the major latex suppliers in Asia, in 1927 Ford had established Fordlandia, a rubber plantation in Brazil (fig. 92). Over 2,500,000 acres of land were cleared along the Tapajoz River (a tributary of the Amazon), and trees were planted to produce latex for automobile tire production at the Rouge. Rivera hoped for stronger relations between South and North America through investments and trade, and he spoke of this panel as a representation of the interdependence of the industrial north and agrarian south: "The ship which transports our products to the tropics and brings their raw materials to us here."[4]

Two Great Lakes freighters (fig. 93) (based on Ford Motor Company ships that carried raw materials from the northern Great Lakes to the Rouge) pass, while race boats and fish glide in front of them (fig. 94). With the industrial port on the left and the rubber tree plantation on the right, the water represents the symbolic confluence of the Detroit and Amazon rivers and represents the interdependence of the Americas. The industrial port is based on the actual boat slip at the Rouge. A pipe-fitter (left) and man working a chain pulley (right) appear in front of a bridge crane on railroad tracks used to unload freighters. The skyline of the city of Detroit is represented in the left background. Water

90. *Interdependence of North and South,* detail of the west wall middle register, fresco. Two Great Lakes freighters (based on Ford Motor Company ships that carried raw materials from the northern Great Lakes to the Rouge) pass, while race boats and fish glide in front of them. With the industrial port on the left and the rubber tree plantation on the right, the water represents the symbolic confluence of the Detroit and Amazon rivers and represents the interdependence of the Americas. The industrial port is based on the actual boat slip at the Rouge. A pipe-fitter (left) and man working a chain pulley (right) appear in front of a bridge crane on railroad tracks used to unload freighters. The skyline of the city of Detroit is represented in the left background. Water tanks, factory smokestacks, the newest skyscraper (the Fisher Building, opened in 1929), and the spire of Saint Anne's Roman Catholic Church are identifiable as some of the city's landmarks.

91. Sketch of entry to the Rouge off Miller Road, 1932, graphite on paper, 15.2 x 22.9 cm. The exteriors of the factories, which incorporated the revolutionary one-story design of Albert Kahn, are introduced into this cityscape. Rivera developed these factories directly from his sketches made at Gate 4 off Miller Road, which shows Power House #1 and the Production Foundry.

tanks, factory smokestacks (fig. 91), the newest skyscraper (the Fisher Building, opened in 1929), and the spire of Saint Anne's Roman Catholic Church are identifiable as some of the city's landmarks. Bertram Wolfe characterized Rivera's desire to paint his utopian ideals in the United States of America as

> an obsession. In a free union of the Americas, in a wedding of the industrial proletariat of the North with the peasantry of the South, of the factories of the United States with the raw materials of Latin America, of the utilitarian aesthetic of the machine with the plastic sense that still inhered in the Amerindian peoples, in the mating of the style which glass and steel and concrete were even then engendering with the style that antique Mexican, Central American, and Peruvian art had begotten on this continent, he foresaw the dawn of a period of new splendors for the continent and for mankind. Increasingly the thought possessed him that he might serve in some small measure to bring about that consummation.[15]

Rivera painted this utopian vision during the height of national antagonism toward Latin America, particularly toward Mexican migrant workers, who in the view of out-of-work Americans during the Depression represented a major threat to their livelihood (see note 45 in Chapter Two).

The coexistence of life and death is graphically presented above the center of the shipping panel, where a half-face and half-skull are painted on either side of a five-pointed star. This dualism is a spiritual concept that goes back to the most ancient beliefs in Mexico. The half-face and half-skull appear throughout ancient Mexican cultures in images as early as Tlatilco sculpture dating from 1000 to 500 B.C. (fig. 89). Rivera described this symbol as "the star, the symbol of life and death since man is ever between the two."[16] The half-face is a portrait of George Washington, whom Rivera referred to as America's first revolutionary.[17] The star in Christian, Middle Eastern, and pre-Columbian iconography generally symbolizes hope. Rivera originally intended the skull to appear in the upper panel that now contains the compass rose. This remnant of pre-Columbian imagery was probably taken from the Mexico City sculpture of Coatlicue, the Aztec goddess of war and creation who is adorned with human hearts and skulls (fig. 185). The sculpture was well known to Rivera. Human sacrifices were made to Coatlicue to insure the continuation of other lives on earth. Rivera may have been thinking of the Aztec equivalent of the Christian Last Judgment theme.

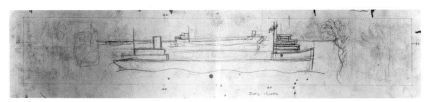

Lower Register: *Steam* and *Electricty*

Vertical panels on each side of the west entrance to the court introduce the theme of the automobile industry through representation of Power House #1 (see figs. 82 and 97). Coal is burned (upper left) to heat water in boilers, creating steam, which is carried by large pipes (lower left) to the giant turbine generator (lower right). The generator produces electricity, which is dispersed to the industrial plants through the control center (upper right).

Rivera saw Power House #1 when new turbine generators were put into operation in July 1932. The Power House was designed and built by the Albert Kahn architectural firm in 1921 and was the principal power generation and distribution facility at the Rouge. It had the world's largest high-pressure boilers and turbines, as well as air compressors, water pumps, a network of electrical transmission lines, steam lines, compressed air lines, mill water lines, drinking water lines, and fire prevention lines (fig. 96).

The elegant form and sensual quality of the industrial power operation are captured in the fresco (fig. 97). In *Steam*, the component parts of the reheat

unit, feeder pipes, passageway, and water pump are rendered to scale, only slightly altered in form, and rearranged to suit the composition of the panel and the vantage point of the viewer. The lower portion of the turbine in the fresco has been altered. Instead of continuing the doughnut shape of the actual machine, Rivera flattened it out to anthropomorphize it into the lobe of a giant ear. Rivera associated the raw energy of steam with the worker and the trans-formed energy of electricity with the manager/engineer. The placement of this ear over the manager/engineer may be Rivera's comment on the strict super-

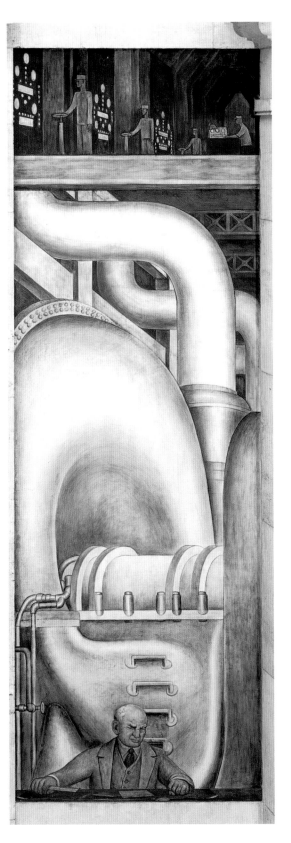

95. Sketch of a worker testing the coal- and gas-burning furnace, which heats the boilers at Power House #1, 1932, charcoal on paper, 15.2 x 22.9 cm.

96. Interior of Power House #1, the Rouge, about 1931.

97. *Steam* and *Electricity*, details of the west wall, fresco. The elegant form and sensual quality of the industrial power operation are captured in the fresco. In the steam panel, the component parts of the reheat unit, feeder pipes, passageway, and water pump are rendered to scale, only slightly altered in form, and rearranged to suit the composition of the panel and the vantage point of the viewer.

98. Sketch of worker studying gauges at Power House #1, 1932, graphite on paper, 15.2 x 22.9 cm.

vision carried out by Ford management, as well as a reference to the deafening noise of the interior of Power House #1. The multiple points of view represented in these panels indicate Rivera's study methods. Climbing into turbines and sketching the steam pipes from different angles and heights, Rivera extended his curiosity beyond the formal qualities of the machines into their functions and sequence of processes (figs. 95, 98). His thorough understanding of the power house operations and their importance to the Rouge is clear.

The manager/engineer in the electricity panel is a composite portrait of

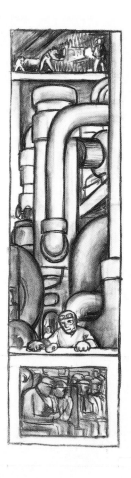

99. Sketch for *Steam* and *Electricity,* 1932, charcoal on tracing paper. These signed and dated sketches indicate that Rivera's ideas for the panels were well developed at an early stage. The two lower panels depicting workers on a lunch break (left) and a trade school class (right) were originally intended to be relief images sculpted by Clifford Wight. They remained part of the design on the walls through the *sinopia* on the brown coat but were later erased to preserve the dado (the lower band of each wall) around the entire court. They appeared in ghost images on the walls until the court was cleaned in 1988.

100 and 101. Sketches for *Steam* and *Electricity,* 1932, charcoal on paper; 51.7 x 14.5 cm. each.

102. Detail of worker/mechanic on the west wall *Steam* panel, fresco. Although the worker/mechanic is not Rivera's true self-portrait, the face and physical build appear to be generalized from the artist's own.

103. Detail of manager/engineer on the west wall *Electricity* panel, fresco.

104. Sketch of worker's gloves, 1932, graphite on paper, 15.2 x 22.9 cm. The worker is wearing gloves bearing the Monte Glove Company's red star insignia on the gauntlet cuffs. Rivera saw many of these gloves throughout the Rouge factories and turned the company logo into a political symbol by including a hammer in the worker's hand to associate him with the communist movement.

105. Thomas Edison and Henry Ford, about 1927. Rivera combined their faces to create the manager/engineer in the fresco.

Henry Ford and Thomas Edison, who were close friends throughout their adult lives. Edison died in 1931 after Ford had already memorialized him by moving the Menlo Park Laboratory, where the electric light was invented, from New Jersey to Greenfield Village. Rivera paid homage to the two men by combining their portraits and placing the figure as a manager/engineer pendant to the communist worker on the opposite side of the entrance (fig. 103). The worker/mechanic is associated with the raw energy of steam (fig. 102). The manager/engineer is associated with the transformed power of electricity. It is ironic that this portrait should represent an engineer reading a blueprint, because Henry Ford distrusted most professionals with formal training (especially engineers, lawyers, and accountants), and he never learned to read a blueprint.

Rivera graphically demonstrates the dichotomy of workers and capitalists in the steam and electricity panels of the west wall. He associates each with different kinds of power but also shows how these forms of power are inextricably linked. In 1922 Henry Ford stated, "It is utterly foolish for Capital or for Labor to think of themselves as groups. They are partners. . . . A great business is really too big to be human. It grows so large as to supplant the personality of man. In a big business, the employer, like the employee is lost in the mass. . . . The business itself becomes a big thing."[18] Rivera shared this point of view and elaborated on it in the automobile panels.

NORTH AND SOUTH WALLS

The north and south walls (figs. 107, 109, and enlargement in pocket) are devoted to representations of the four races, the automobile industry (fig. 109), and the secondary industries of Detroit—medicine, drugs, gas bomb production, and commercial chemicals. They continue the themes established on the east and west walls which combine ancient and Christian symbolic systems. The organization of each wall follows a pattern: monumental figures on top, the workers' everyday world of the factories in the center, and small monochrome panels showing a day in the life of a worker on the lower edge. The latter are reminiscent of the predella panels of Italian Renaissance altarpieces, which contained a border under the main images and depicted scenes in the life of the religious figure represented above. The walls also recall Mexican *retablos* and ex-voto paintings, created to celebrate the successful healing of an individual. These tiny works on tin were painted by artists for hire, who would translate the verbal description of a miraculous event into images. They usually depict the deity on the top and the person who is sick in the middle; a description of the event in words or tiny scenes illustrating the healing process appears on the lower register of the composition.

North and South Walls: The Four Races Panels

Rivera monumentalized the format: the four races take the position of the deity, the interiors of the factories take the place of the victim who is healed, and the small monochrome panels of a day in the life of a worker take the place of the description of the event.

Rivera elevates the worker to majestic scale. Not only does he place the four races at the top of the hierarchy of the work force, but he associates with them the four basic elements used in making steel (figs. 111, 112, 114, 115). The figures of the races hold raw materials that Rivera saw as analogous to each race "in their plastic quality of color and form, as well as by their historic functions."[19] "The figures represent the four elements most important in making steel. They are coal, iron ore, sand, and lime. Here there is an aesthetic as well as a literary analogy in making the black race represent coal; the yellow race, sand; the red race, iron, and the white race, lime."[20] Each idealized type is predestined to play a prescribed role in the chemistry of society, just as coal, sand, iron, and lime each serve roles for the making of steel. It was common practice to assign stereotypical racial characteristics, and Rivera's intention was to describe each race positively. He also assigned characteristics to the culture of each race. To Rivera, the yellow race is the oldest and most numerous and thus it is compared to sand, which is used in making molds for steel. The red race was the first in the Americas and thus is like iron ore, whose crystals reminded him of Indian decoration. The black race's aesthetic sense is like fire and its labor represents the hard strength that carbon in coal gives to steel. Carbon under pressure produces diamonds. The white race has a disciplined structural character and is the organizer of the world, which, like lime, brings other agents together, as in the making of steel.[21]

Rivera's Chapingo Chapel murals and Michelangelo's Sistine Chapel ceiling have both been cited as inspiration for the four races murals in Detroit.[22] Michelangelo's figures of Adam and the *ignudi* may have inspired the Chapingo reclining nudes. The major reclining nudes there are based on portraits of Rivera's then wife, Guadalupe Marin, and his mistress, the photographer Tina Modotti. However, their placement as single figures on two walls, their sensuality, and the specificity of sex and individual features are far from the androgynous generalized figures of the four races in Detroit. The Detroit figures are

somewhat awkwardly placed in their rectangular spaces. Their torsos face squarely front, while the legs appear at right angles to the torsos. The foreshortening of each body is exaggerated to such an extent that the legs appear as miniature appendages. The real power of the figures emanates from their weighty quality and their facial features, painted in a highly sculptural fashion as if chiseled in stone.

The four races are close in form and function to the Chac Mool sculptures used as sacrificial stones in Aztec and Toltec death rituals. While the Chac Mool reclines on his back, the body is viewed in profile from the front and the face is at right angles to it, looking out toward the viewer full face. The sculptures retain the blocklike quality of the stones out of which they are carved. The figures, dressed as warriors, are messengers who bring the hearts of human victims to the gods.[23] In the four races, the sacrifice is not one of human hearts to keep the universe functioning but of human and mechanical energy as well as nature's raw materials used to make steel. The races are thus the intermediaries between the energy sacrificed by the workers and given to the universe.

Gigantic hands emerge from a volcano on the north wall and from a stepped pyramid on the south wall (figs. 111, 112, 114, 115). They grasp metals used in the production of steel—manganese, nickel, tungsten, and molybdenum—and thus symbolize mining in particular and the aggressive human drive to capture the riches of the earth in general.[24] Rivera had originally wanted to paint mining scenes on the top registers of the court, "but it was impossible to do that because the pattern of the mines would be too crowded in so narrow a space. So the wealth of the mines is represented by monumental figures. They are large not only to fill the space, but because they represent the large masses of ore in the earth."[25]

Monumental disembodied hands first appear in Rivera's murals at Chapingo. Two, each painted in a lunette on the left wall of the chapel, correspond directly to the hands in the Detroit murals and carry explicit meaning. Each hand at Chapingo is above a panel illustrating the stages of social revolution. The first in the sequence is an open left hand with palm forward titled *Beginning of Warfare*. It appears above the scene of *Underground Organization of the Agrarian Movement*, where "a young agrarian leader exhorts farmers and their families to

106. Sketch for the north and east walls, 1932, graphite on paper, 20.3 x 25.4 cm.

following pages:

107. North wall, fresco: *The Red and Black Races*, 2.69 x 13.72 m.; *Geological Strata*, 1.33 x 13.72 m.; *Manufacture of Poisonous Gas Bombs*, 2.58 x 2.13 m.; *Vaccination*, 2.58 x 2.13 m.; *Cells Suffocated by Poisonous Gas*, .68 x 1.85 m.; *Healthy Human Embryo*, .68 x 1.85 m.; *Production and Manufacture of Engine and Transmission (Ford V-8)*, 5.40 x 13.72 m.

108. Diagram of north wall.

109. South wall, fresco: *The White and Yellow Races*, 2.69 x 13.72 m.; *Geological Strata*, 1.33 x 13.72 m.; *Pharmaceutics*, 2.58 x 2.13 m.; *Commercial Chemical Operations*, 2.58 x 2.13 m.; *Surgery*, .68 x 1.85 m.; *Crystals*, .68 x 1.85 m.; *Production of Automobile Exterior and Final Assembly*, 5.40 x 13.72 m.

110. Diagram of south wall.

93

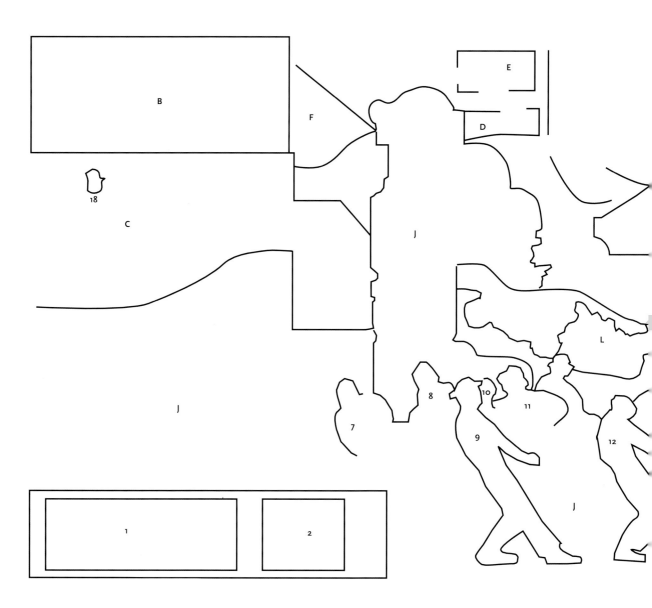

108. Diagram of north wall automotive panel: *Production and Manufacture of Engine and Transmission.*

Iron and steel production operations:

A. Blast furnace and open hearth furnace.

Production foundry operations:

B. Making mold patterns.

C. Right—mixing sand for molds; left—packing sand into mold cores.

D. Hammering plugs into molds.

E. Securing tops on casting boxes.

F. Casting boxes put on table-height conveyor.

G. Casting boxes put on overhead conveyor to cupola furnaces in foundry.

H. Molten steel from cupola being poured into casting boxes from ladles.

I. Chippers and sand blasting taking rough edges off newly cast engine blocks.

J. Drilling and honing operations of engine block. Right—two men adjusting V-shaped honing machine; four men steadying machine cover suspended by chains from crane operator's box. Right and left center—two rows of multiple spindles. Left—men on line carrying out deburring operations. Center—engine blocks being lifted from conveyor to transfer table and taken to motor assembly plant.

K. Foundry and drilling operations of the transmission housing

Motor Assembly Plant Operations:

L. Motor assembly: men attaching cylinder head covers and smaller parts to engine block.

M. Gear silent test, layout and connecting rod inspections.

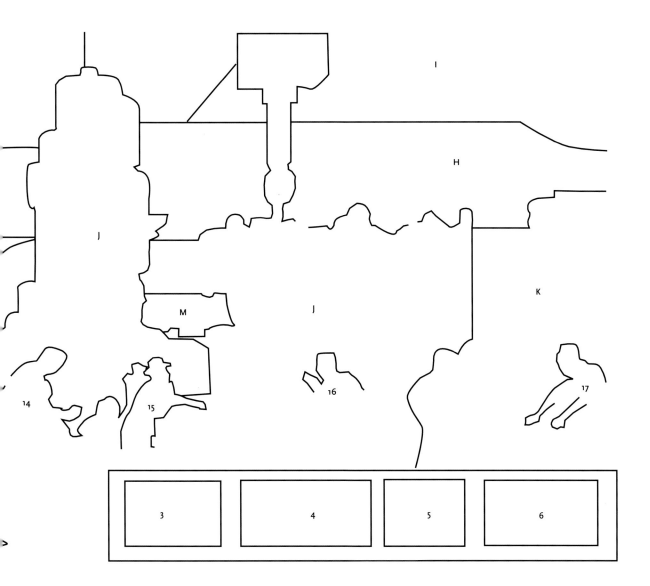

Predella Panels:

1. Open hearth operations entrance: workers punch in at time clock.

2. Open hearth operations: molten metal being poured into ingot molds.

3. Rolling Mill: ingots being transferred by buggy to reheat furnaces before rolling.

4. Billet Mill: ingots being rolled into bars.

5. Bar Mill: metal bars being piled and cut.

6. Tandem Mill: lunch break.

Portraits:

7. Stephen Pope Dimitroff, assistant to Rivera.

8. Arthur S. Niendorf, assistant to Rivera.

9. Detroit acquaintance of Rivera.

10. Clifford Wight, chief assistant to Rivera.

11. Harry Glicksman, Ford employee.

12. Arthur S. Niendorf (see Portrait 8).

13. Joseph Spinney, museum gardener.

14. Paul Boatin, Detroit acquaintance of Rivera.

15. Andres Sanchez Flores, chemist to Rivera.

16. Ford engineer.

17. John Bauer, museum guard, Henry Ford's schoolmate.

18. Diego Rivera.

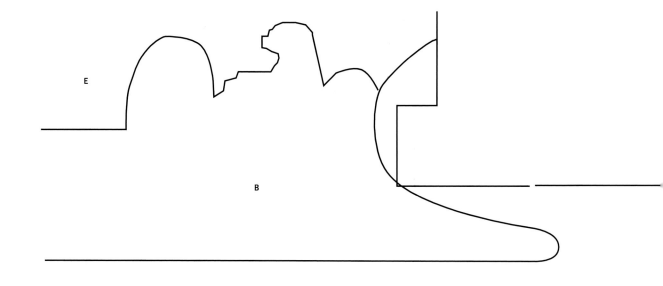

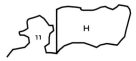

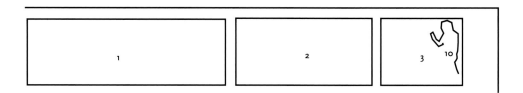

110. Diagram of south wall automotive panel: *Production of Automobile Exterior and Final Assembly.*

Pressed Steel Building Operations (now Dearborn Stamping Plant):
A. Center—fender stamping press. Lower left—spot and seam welders.
B. Top portion of stamping presses.

B Building (now Dearborn Assembly Plant):
C. Left to right—steam pipe fitter fixing air valve; bumpers and grinders working on body panels.
D. Welding buck.
E. Painters.
F. Final assembly.
G. Women testing spark plugs and ignition systems.
H. Constant temperature testing room.

Spring and Upset Building:
I. Heat-treating furnace, where metal bars are heated to be shaped into automobile parts.

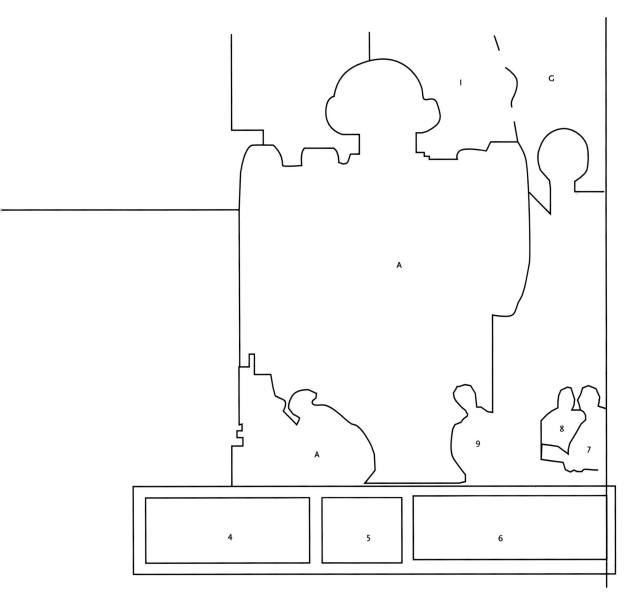

Predella panels:

1. By-Products Building—fertilizer operations.

2. Spring and Upset Building—making parts to repair machines.

3. B Building—trade school engine class led by Henry Ford.

4. Glass Plant—rolling operations.

5. Glass Plant—polishing and stacking operations.

6. Gate 4 pedestrian walkway (overpass) at Miller Road connecting Production Foundry with facade of Motor Assembly Plant to parking lots. Workers, paid at armored truck, take the walkway to bus stops and parking lots.

Portraits:

7. Dr. William Valentiner, director of the Detroit Institute of Arts.

8. Edsel B. Ford, president of the Arts Commission and donor.

9. Ernst Halberstadt, artist assistant to Diego Rivera.

10. Henry Ford.

11. M. L. Bricker, assistant to Henry Ford in charge of production.

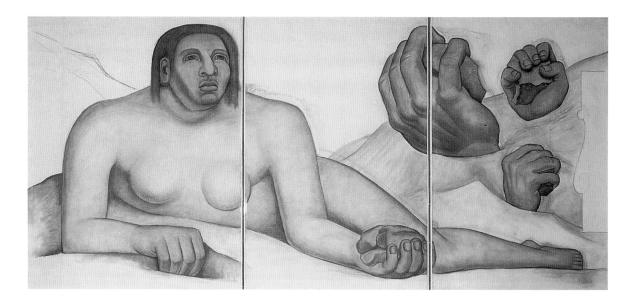

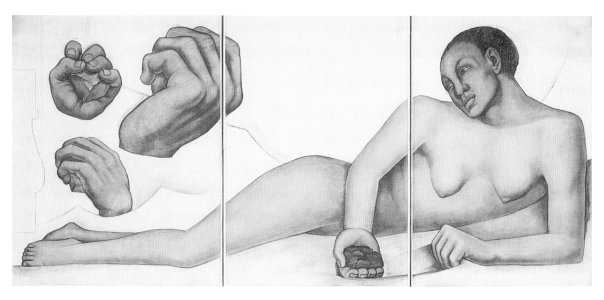

111. *The Red Race,* 1932, cartoon for north wall, brown and red pigment with charcoal over light charcoal, 2.70 x 5.85 m.

112. *The Black Race,* 1932, cartoon for north wall, brown and red pigment with charcoal over light charcoal, 2.64 x 5.82 m. The model for the black race was the Riveras' maid at their apartment in the Wardell Hotel. Her name has not been found.

113. Sketch for south wall races panel, 1932, charcoal on paper, 20.3 x 25.4 cm.

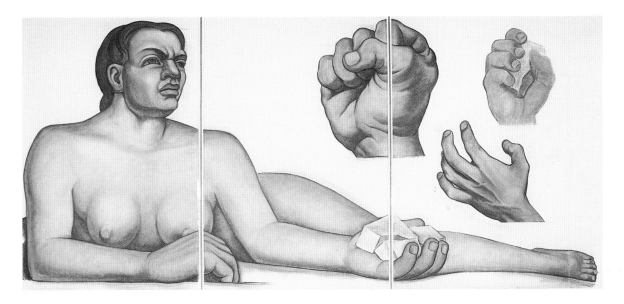

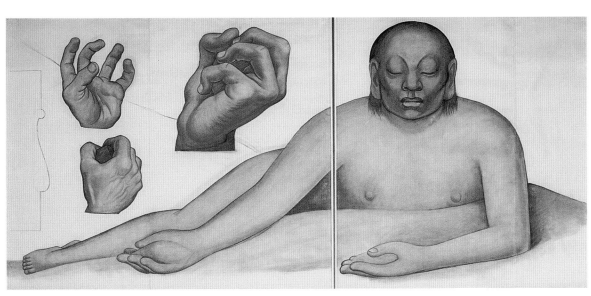

rebel."[26] The leader's role is as propagandist, symbolically dropping the seeds of ideas to germinate in the workers' minds.[27] "In perfect synthesis, a hand, slightly open as though it had just tossed the seed of a great idea to the wind, promises and convinces."[28] The open hand on the left in the *Detroit Industry* south wall races panel is identical to the one in *Beginning of Warfare*, except it is seen from the reverse; the back of the hand faces the viewer. The open hand on the right of the south wall races panel in Detroit is a left hand, palm forward. It, too, is also almost identical to the one at Chapingo. The open hands in Detroit probably carry the same meaning they do in Chapingo—that of distributing the seeds of revolution—as well as representing miners. The second hand at Chapingo, a right-handed fist titled *Resolution,* appears over the panel *Continuous Renewal of Revolutionary Struggle,* which depicts the death and burial of a young leader, whose sacrifice causes the tree overhead to flower.[29] Sacrifice leads to redemptive power. While there are fists holding rocks on both races panels in Detroit, the only empty fist appears in the south wall. It is right-handed and, unlike the palm-forward fist at Chapingo, is rotated to a three-quarter view, squarely confronting the figure of the white race (fig. 114, above). Rivera implied that the forceful resolution of the continuing revolutionary struggle is only necessary against one race. The third hand in the sequence in Chapingo, an open right hand with outstretched fingers—an allusion to the Christian sign of benediction—is titled *The Rightness of the New*

114. *The White Race,* 1932, cartoon for south wall, brown and red pigment with charcoal over light charcoal, 2.71 x 5.84 m. The model for the white race was Lucienne Bloch.

115. *The Yellow Race,* 1932, cartoon for south wall, brown and red pigment with charcoal over light charcoal, 2.69 x 5.82 m. All the faces have an immediacy of expression captured by a fluid drawing technique and brushed-on dry pigment. The undulating lines of the torsos and legs in the cartoons are in contrast to the blocklike quality of the forms in the fresco. Large, disembodied hands are drawn in each cartoon. The cartoons do not include the pyramid or volcano of the frescoes.

Rivera intended the cartoons to be works of art in themselves, as can be seen from the finished degree of execution.

116. *The Red and Black Races* and *Geological Strata*, detail of the north wall, fresco. In order to deepen the blue of the sky above the black race, Rivera painted over it after the plaster had dried.

Order.[30] It does not have an equivalent in Detroit. But the "new order" had not yet appeared in the industrialized north. The industrial revolution of technology had occurred in Detroit, but the social revolution was just beginning.

Rivera linked the volcano (fig. 116) with the pyramid (fig. 117) and with the blast furnace, a mechanical volcano two registers below, in the north wall automotive panel (fig. 107). Just as the raw power of steam is associated with the worker and electricity with the manager/inventor on the west wall, the black and red races are associated with the naturally formed mountain and the white and yellow races relate to the pyramid, a man-made mountain. This is a mixed metaphor, since pyramids were constructed by the indigenous people of Latin America, not by the white or yellow races. However, it is an example of Rivera's ability to connect analogous images and concepts. What was important to Rivera was that all four races share an indigenous cultural and technological heritage in the Americas.

The importance of the volcano lies in its fiery interior. This establishes another theme related to the cardinal points of the compass. The north, with its absence of light, represents the interior and spiritual nature of the universe. Note that the volcano is not erupting in Detroit. The erupting volcano in the Palacio Nacional stairway panel *The Aztec World* painted in 1929 signifies the coming "destruction of the pre-Spanish world."[31] The eruption in Detroit takes place in the man-made volcano—the blast furnace—where the new age of technology exists. The importance of the pyramid lies in its exterior, a monumental link to the heavens. The sun-filled south represents the exterior and material nature of the universe. The color of the races corresponds to the wall of light (south) and wall of darkness (north); the light-colored races are represented on the south wall and the dark-colored races are on the north wall. The volcano and pyramid also emphasize the dual realities of life—the interior and exterior, the natural and spiritual, the inner-directed and outward-directed.

North and South Walls: *Geological Strata* Panels

Below the four races panels, Rivera painted geological cross-sections showing iron ore (hematite) under the red race, coal with fossils and diamonds under the black race, limestone under the white race, and sand and fossils under the yellow race, each with appropriate crystals (figs. 116, 117). As discussed above, Rivera saw the raw materials as analogous to racial characteristics. Billions of years of geological formation are telescoped into each image. Rivera painted the igneous rocks (iron ore and coal) on the north wall and the sedimentary rocks (limestone and sand) on the south wall. He painted the hematite crystals hovering over four volcanic cones within a lake bed of iron compound, silt, and sand. The most important iron ore deposits in the United States lie near Lake Superior in Minnesota and Michigan. The Ford Motor Company had iron ore reserves in the Upper Peninsula of Michigan at this time.[32]

The hematite in the mural is depicted in distinct shapes that correspond to the ancient Greek concept of the elements as represented by five perfect solids: earth equals cube; fire equals tetrahedron; air equals octahedron; ether equals dodecahedron; and water equals icosahedron.[33]

Coal (or carbon) is used to generate electricity and to make coke, an ingredient in the production of iron and steel. The coal in the north wall fresco is shown densely layered between fossilized bogs of ferns and treelike plants. The volcanic derivation of iron ore and diamonds is signified by the image of molten lava in the middle of the north wall middle panel. The lava also connects the volcano to the blast furnace, which returns these materials to a molten state to make steel. The diamond relates to the character of the black race (which in Rivera's view was also developed under great social pressure); it also directly refers to the drilling process shown below in the automotive panel, since diamonds are used in industry to cut, grind, and bore hard metals quickly and accurately.

117. *The White and Yellow Races* and *Geological Strata,* detail of the south wall, fresco.

The representation of the north wall volcano and the south wall pyramid places the four races on sacred ground—one a natural formation, the other built from blocks of hardened lava, both symbolically linking the earth to the heavens. The volcano is nature's equivalent of the blast furnace that is painted directly below it in the north automotive panel. While the notion of the American melting pot, where all races would meld into a new race, was prevalent in the 1930s, Rivera's physical separation of the four races and the distinct characterizations given according to the natural properties of raw materials does not reinforce this concept. However, the depictions of the automobile factories in which all races work together does approach this analogy.

On the south wall middle panel (fig. 117) Rivera painted a stratum of limestone. Fine-grained limestone is represented by white blocks in five even layers. Coquina limestone, formed from shells and corals that have ingested calcium carbonate, is depicted as layers of sand. Coquina is used in buildings and road construction. The crystal formation on the left is calcite, a chief source of lime used in producing glass and steel and in fresco making. The plaster walls on which the Detroit frescoes were painted are a combination of calcite and sand.

On the right of the south wall middle panel is a depiction of fossils with quartz crystals, the most common mineral in sand. Silica, a pure form of quartz sand, is used for manufacturing glass and making molds, both of which are represented in the north and south automotive panels. Sand, as we have seen, is also a basic ingredient in fresco making. The geological strata are painted in wavelike patterns that give visual life to the images and symbolic life to the inorganic materials. Mineral crystals are nonorganic substances that grow. Rivera saw a basic synergistic relationship between the inorganic and organic, the raw materials of the earth and their basis in mineral, biological, and industrial materials. "These same chemical elements which go into the making of steel, we also

find in the animal and vegetable elements, and in the cells of the human body, and so I put those cells here to represent the unity of all life as it is derived from the earth, and the constant cycle of destruction and construction which is essential to all growth."[34]

To Rivera, the wave was the visual analogy of the transmission and transformation of energy. "Rivera had always been intrigued by the image of the wave. Increasingly it had been implicit in his painting. . . . Now he set out to paint the wave explicitly, the wave that runs through electrons, mountains, water, wind, life, death, the seasons, sound, light, that does not cease to undulate in the dead, nor in things that have never lived."[35] Wave theory, rooted in late nineteenth- and early twentieth-century physics, explained the movement of pure energy or light and had assisted in refuting the French chemist Louis Pasteur's hypothesis of the 1860s that life arises only from other life. As revived by the Russian physicist Aleksander Ivanovich Oparin (1894–1980) and others in the 1920s, it was favored by intellectual circles in Rivera's time to demonstrate the unity of life: "life arises spontaneously from nonliving matter with the qualification that extremely long periods of time (millions of years) under the right conditions on a primitive earth were involved."[36] Theosophists such as Annie Besant and Walter Russell expanded on the scientific theory of light to explain the movement of energy as a divine principle found in everything on earth. Elie Faure, a physician and art connoisseur who was Rivera's mentor during his Paris years, introduced him to the theosophical ideas of Madame Blavatsky. Rivera may have been aware of Russell's writings, which were first published in 1926, or he could have met him or heard him lecture at the Artists League of New York, of which Russell was president in the early 1930s. "In the Wave lies the secret of Creation. All energy is expressed in motion. All motion is expressed in waves. All energy is reproduced, or transferred, or transmitted, by impact of energy against inertia."[37]

118. *Manufacture of Poisonous Gas Bombs,* 1932, cartoon for the north wall, charcoal, 2.55 x 2.19 m.

119. *Worker with Gas Mask,* 1932, black chalk, 15.2 x 22.9 cm.

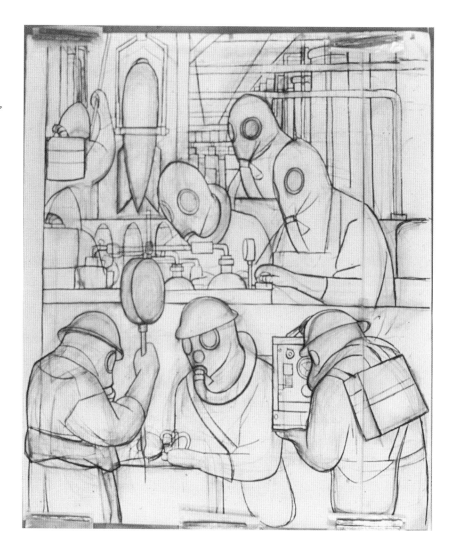

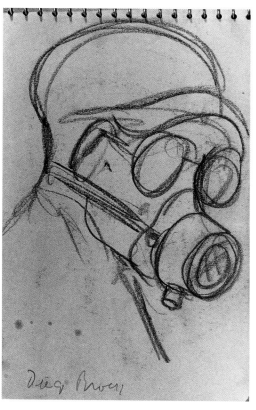

120. *Manufacture of Poisonous Gas Bombs* and *Cells Suffocated by Poisonous Gas,* detail of the north wall, fresco. This shows the destructive side of chemical technology. Eight figures in gas masks are working with chemicals (the operation has been identified as the making of a bromide or a chloride). Chloride had been used in gas bombs in World War I; these were the most feared weapons of war at that time. In the foreground, the figure at left holds a temperature gauge, the one in the center holds a storage drum, and the one on the right is working with a potentiometer, an electrical resistance measuring device used to measure current and temperature. In the middle ground, three figures are working with standard chemical apparatus and glassware to fill casings with gas. In the background, a figure with his back toward the viewer watches another hoist a loaded gas bomb by a pulley between rows of blow-out towers (used in bromide production). The image is made chilling and ominous by the bomb and the hovering depersonalized figures in their insectlike masks.

In the lower panel, cells are suffocated by poison gas. The poison gas here is created when high sulfur content coal is burned and the sulfur dioxide that is produced is combined with water. The panel includes a pile of coal with the sulfuric acid billowing up and around images of cells as seen under a microscope. Rivera was aware that sulfuric acid produced by burning industrial coal was a major health hazard not only for workers but for everyone who breathed the air.

North and South Wall Corner Panels: *Manufacture of Poisonous Gas Bombs, Vaccination, Pharmaceutics,* and *Commercial Chemical Operations*

On both sides of the four races panels on the north and south walls, Rivera painted corner panels that serve as visual parentheses to the gigantic figures (figs. 120, 122). They continue the themes of the unity of organic and inorganic life and the constructive and destructive uses of technology. The north wall right corner panel depicts a child being vaccinated. Below the vaccination panel, a healthy human embryo is shown gaining sustenance from the geological strata and at the same time being threatened by microscopic images of diseases (fig. 122). On the left corner is a depiction of the production of gas bombs. The small panel below it shows a microscopic view of cells being attacked and destroyed by poisonous gases (fig. 120).

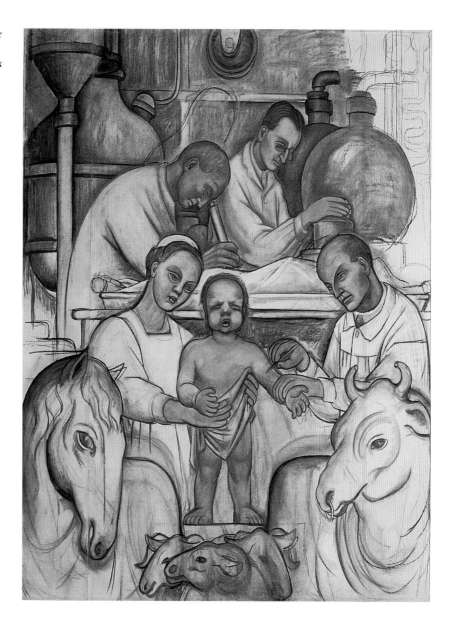

121. *Vaccination*, 1932, cartoon for the north wall, charcoal with red pigment over light charcoal, 2.55 x 2.20 m.

The south wall left corner panel represents a pharmaceutics laboratory (fig. 131). A chemist/businessman in the center is surrounded by women sorting pills. In the small panel below the *Pharmaceutics* panel, surgery on an animal is taking place. Animal organs used to create drugs surround the surgery scene. On the right corner panel is a commercial chemical operations scene; in the panel below it, sulfur crystals are mixed with water to produce a gas (fig. 133).

Rivera could have seen large-scale commercial chemical operations both at the Detroit Chemical Company and at the Dow Chemical Company in nearby Midland, Michigan. While commercial chemical plants would have produced the gases used in gas bombs, they did not make the casings for the bombs themselves. Rivera combined two major operations in one. Considering the detailed rendering of the bomb casing, Rivera must have seen gas bomb production either in person or in photographs.

North Wall *Vaccination* Panel: "Into the fight between construction and destruction come the chemists and scientists in Detroit making their vaccines, so in one picture they are depicted in a panel of a little child surrounded by white-coated doctors and nurses, with the cattle brought here from which the vaccines are made" (fig. 122).[38] Rivera presents, on one level, scientific research and its application to prevent smallpox. The beneficiary is a young child who will be

122. *Vaccination* and *Healthy Human Embryo,* detail of the north wall, fresco. In the *Vaccination* panel, a child is vaccinated by a doctor, who is attended by a nurse. In the foreground are a horse, a sheep, and a cow. Vaccines are made in the background by three scientists in a dissection laboratory. The composition of this panel is directly taken from the Italian Renaissance form of the nativity, where the bibilical figures of Mary and Joseph and Jesus are depicted in the foreground and the three wise men in the background. The three wise men are scientists who dissect dogs for the benefit of human health.

The *Healthy Human Embryo* sac is surrounded by an egg. Sperm, multiplying chromosomes, red and white blood cells, and six forms of bacteria (tetanus, typhoid, diptheria, cholera, tuberculosis, and an unidentified tetracoccus) are associated with the work of the three scientists in the vaccination panel.

immune to the disease. Dorothy McMeekin believes that the scientists in the background are symbolic representations of Pasteur, Elie Metchnikoff (1845–1916), and Robert Koch (1843–1910), three Nobel Prize–winning scientists who developed vaccines, made important studies of white blood cells that attack diseases, developed bacteriology as a science, and discovered the germ that causes tuberculosis, respectively.[39] Lucienne Bloch's diary records that the three scientists represent a Catholic, a Protestant, and a Jew, or ecumenical wise men who bring the gifts of science to the child.

Stephen Dimitroff identified the portraits in the *Vaccination* panel as based on likenesses of Jean Harlow (the nurse), Dr. William Valentiner (the doctor, fig. 124), and Charles A. Lindbergh, Jr. (the child, fig. 123)—an unlikely combination of people to appear in a traditional form of a nativity. But all these people

123. Charles Augustus Lindbergh, Jr., *Time*, May 2, 1932. This kidnapped child's image served as the model for the baby in the *Vaccination* panel.

124. *Portrait of William R. Valentiner*, 1932, red chalk and pencil, 68.6 x 53.5 cm. Rivera had Valentiner pose for him on May 24, 1932, just a few days before the director went to Europe on leave for several months.

> Today Rivera made a sketch of me in profile, with finest red and black chalk. While other artists usually waste a lot of paper, he only used one Sheet. With the greatest assurance he drew the outlines with fine and even Lines. It was at its best, when after half an hour the sketch was finished. I was flattered when at first he thought I looked like Erasmus of Rotterdam. Later he thought I had a Renaissance head, good for modeling. I sat for my portrait one and a half hours before and one and a half hours after lunch. Tomorrow morning he only wants to add a few lines.[43]

The portrait of Valentiner is inscribed "*A mon cher ami M. William Valentiner./Diego Rivera 1932.*" It remained in the director's collection throughout his life. Rivera used the portrait twice: as inspiration for the doctor in *Vaccination* and as the basis for the director's portrait in the style of a Renaissance patron next to Edsel B. Ford on the south wall automotive panel.

were significant to the artist. The Lindbergh child was kidnapped on March 1, 1932, when Rivera was in New York after his successful one-man exhibition at the Museum of Modern Art and preparing to go to Detroit. For ten weeks the Lindbergh kidnapping was in the media while a search was conducted and negotiations went on with the kidnappers, until the child's body was found. Rivera and Kahlo had become acquainted with Anne Morrow Lindbergh and Charles Lindbergh in 1929 when Anne's father, Dwight Morrow, who was then United States Ambassador to Mexico, commissioned Rivera to paint a mural in Cuernavaca.

E. P. Richardson, recalled that the artist "was consciously thinking about the Holy Family, not in a religious sense, but as one of the ancient archetypes of human relationships—man, woman and child—and the pursuit of wise men, the pursuit of knowledge for the benefit of mankind, and the protection of the child against disease and ill. . . . He had a strong sense of archetypal relationships in human life."[40] It is clear that the artist had an Italian Renaissance nativity scene in mind when painting this panel (fig. 127).

North Wall *Healthy Human Embryo* Panel: The small panel below the *Vaccination* panel depicts a healthy human embryo suspended in amniotic fluid and receiving nourishment from the geological strata and crystals through the umbilical cord (fig. 122). Rivera's accurate representation of chromosomes indicates his understanding of their significance in the scientific debate at that time regarding their role in heredity.[41] "Rivera knew nothing about DNA and Transfer and Messenger [since they had not yet been postulated in the 1930s] and yet his thinking process, the use of analogy, led him to a rough mental image that is very like the working model for the control of cellular development that is used today."[42] McMeekin makes a compelling argument for Rivera's having drawn a compositional analogy between cell reproduction in the *Healthy Human Embryo* panel and the manufacture of the automobile body in the south wall automotive panel.

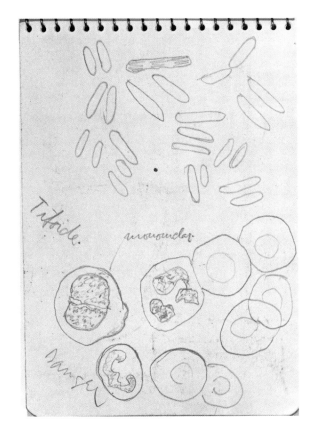

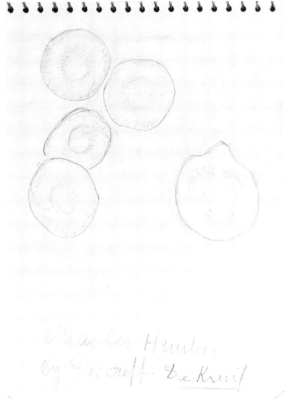

125. Sketch of typhoid bacteria, 1932, graphite on paper, 15.2 x 22.9 cm. Rivera sent Ernst Halberstadt to one of the city's downtown hospitals to make sketches of the dissection room and laboratory equipment and to bring back a microscope and slides of cells as well as medical reference books. Rivera used these sketches and slides for the four medical panels in the murals—*Vaccination* on the north wall, and *Pharmaceutics* on the south wall, and the small panels below each of them. He later used them in the Rockefeller Center mural and the Museo de Bellas Artes murals in Mexico City. Rivera's sketchbook drawings include microscopic images of diptheria and typhoid organisms labeled in Spanish.

126. Sketch of microscopic cells with inscription "*Microbe Hunters*, De Kruif," pencil and graphite on paper, 15.2 x 22.9 cm. Lucienne Bloch remembered the Riveras' apartment as filled with medical and scientific texts. *Microbe Hunters* is a classic text on the history of microbiology.

127. Preliminary sketch for *Vaccination*, graphite on paper, 21.6 x 27.9 cm.

128. *Pharmaceutics*, 1932, cartoon for the south wall, charcoal 2.54 x 2.20 m. The cartoon of the *Pharmaceutics* panel predicts the final fresco in every detail except for a very large outlined left-handed fist that emerges from the bottom of the paper in front of the dissecting pans and the chemist/manager's pill-sorting machine. This fist is identical to the one in the adjacent panel poised toward the white race. The cartoon may have been pinned in place on the wall and then used for sketching the fist for the upper south panel of the south wall while Rivera was painting the central register.

129. Martin Schongauer, German, about 1450–1491, *The Tribulations of Saint Anthony*, about 1470–1475, engraving.

130. Ben Shahn, American, 1898–1969, *Father Coughlin*, 1939, brush, wash, ink, and watercolor on paper, 39.4 x 30.5 cm.

Rivera not only made analogies between organic and inorganic systems but also believed in their essential connection. For example, in speaking about the effects of art on people, he thought that these were as important as those of the digestive system and worked in a similar way. "A work of art is an agent capable of producing definite physiological phenomena, perfectly precise, or glandular secretions—notably from the suprarenal gland which provides the human organism with elements as necessary to human life as are those which the digestive system extracts by means of the phenomenon of ingestion, mastication, digestion, etc. So, in reality art is a vital necessity for the human being."[44] Thus the interdependency of the fetus and inorganic material is obvious to Rivera. And their placement on the same level as the geological strata is no coincidence.

South Wall *Pharmaceutics* Panel: The south wall left corner panel represents the pharmaceutics industry (fig. 131). *Pharmaceutics* is based on drawings of the Parke-Davis pharmaceutics firm in Detroit. The figure in the foreground represents the chemist/manager, who is surrounded by devices such as a pill sorter, an adding machine on top of a Gothic-styled radio, a microphone, and a telephone. The panel is dominated by this figure, which was based on the likeness of Homer C. Fritsch, an executive vice-president at Parke-Davis (fig. 132).[45] Women sorting pills surround the manager. In the background, drying ovens and chemical operations are shown.

There is an odd quality to this panel that Bertram Wolfe and others have explained by citing its "mischievous allusion to the 'Temptation of Saint Anthony' scene" (fig. 129).[46] Here the modern "saint" is surrounded by full-

131. *Pharmaceutics* and *Surgery*, detail of the south wall, fresco. *Pharmaceutics* is based on drawings of the Parke-Davis pharmaceutics firm in Detroit. The figure in the foreground represents the chemist/manager, who is surrounded by devices such as a pill sorter, an adding machine on top of a Gothic-styled radio, a microphone, and a telephone.

132. Homer C. Fritch, executive vice-president, Parke-Davis, about 1950. He served as model for the chemist/manager.

bodied women with exposed knees and calves. There is great contrast between the diminutive, bald-headed manager totally absorbed in running the business and the buxom young women surrounding him on both sides and above his head. But the temptresses are as unconscious of their allure as the saint is not noticeably tempted, other than to give an occasional glance to check on them through his rearview mirror. What Rivera has presented here is a person so absorbed in business that he has lost part of his humanity.

The microphone and the radio, with its Gothic design, may allude to the broadcasts aired regularly from the Shrine of the Little Flower, a Roman Catholic Church in Royal Oak, a few miles north of Detroit. Father Charles Edward Coughlin (1891–1971) reigned there as a priest of the radical right wing who railed against the liberal practices in the city and country in the 1930s (fig. 130).

For many months after the controversy erupted over the murals, Father Coughlin was an outspoken opponent of them. The appearance of the microphone demonstrates Rivera's fascination with technology and his warnings about its proper uses.

South Wall *Surgery* Panel: The small panel below the *Pharmaceutics* panel depicts brain surgery in the center, surrounded by human organs and the same four geological elements found in the middle registers—iron, coal, limestone, and sand. Above the gloved hands is a view of an open skull. The right hand of the surgeon has just extracted a brain tumor. Rivera divided the organs between those of reproduction on the right and digestion on the left. McMeekin sees here an allusion to the French novelist Emile Zola's mystical ideas of the function of the stomach and sexual organs, "where the germs of future generations were elaborated," and to the scientific ideas of Zola's friend the pioneer physiologist Claude Bernard and other scientists, who advanced scientific understanding of the role of organs, as well as the knowledge of hormones, control of diabetes with insulin, and nutritional diseases.[47]

On the upper right side of *Surgery* (fig. 131), male and female sexual glands are represented: fallopian tube, uterus, mammary gland, testis, vas deferens, seminal vesicle, and prostate gland; along with a bladder and suprarenal glands. Digestive organs are presented on the left: small intestine, gallbladder, pancreas, intussusception, with the blood supply to the esophagus, and a thyroid gland.[48] In the lower foreground the artist painted three covered dissecting trays (identical to one bearing a dog in the *Vaccination* panel).

It was in the fall of 1932 that the artist painted the middle-register panels *Cells Suffocated by Poisonous Gas, Infant in the Bulb of a Plant, Healthy Human Embryo,* and *Surgery*—soon after Kahlo's miscarriage (fig. 59), the death of her mother, and the beginning of a disastrous diet of citrus fruit and vegetable juice Rivera put himself on.[49] He was intensely occupied with life and death, science and doctors, reproductive and digestive organs, and homeopathic and pharmaceutic remedies (fig. 125). The scientific books in the Riveras' Detroit apartment served the personal and professional needs of both (fig. 126). For Kahlo, the texts helped her understand her own anatomy during her pregnancy. After the miscarriage, she transformed the genre of scientific illustration in her art. For Rivera, the medical and scientific texts served to link macrocosmic ideas of the interdependency of the biological, mineral, and technological worlds. The ordered universe in the frescoes was in contrast to personal physical realities— the complications of Diego's own rebellious, corpulent body and his ineffective remedies, as well as Frida's miscarriage due to a damaged skeleton and reproductive organs from an accident many years before.

South Wall *Commercial Chemical Operations* Panel: The right corner panel, *Commercial Chemical Operations* (fig. 133), may depict a magnesium cell operation or perhaps an ammonia operation. If this is a magnesium cell operation, the two men are ladling molten metal. If they are holding a scraper, they are working at an oven heating coal to recover ammonia and coal tar products.[50] The panel is stylistically and compositionally the most sophisticated of the upper panels. It is painted in a futurist style to demonstrate the movement of the workers, showing them in two different positions. Rivera met the artist Gino Severini and became familiar with the futurist style of painting in Italy during a sojourn there in 1919 and 1920. Use of this style is rare in Rivera's work. It is used effectively here to illustrate up-and-down movement and conveys a modernism that

133. *Commercial Chemical Operations* and *Sulphur and Potash*, detail of the south wall, fresco. The figure in the lower left holds a torch to heat substances in the drums. In the left background a man in a lab coat works with standard chemical apparatus at a table. Behind him a workman studies gauges probably related to the ovens. In the upper right a man may be working on a brine well drilling process. In the far background, beyond criss-crossing steel girders painted red, are two figures ascending stairs.

matches the subject portrayed. This panel differs dramatically from *The Red and Black Races* panel on the north wall (the first panel to be painted in this register, fig. 107). In the *Races* panel, the composition is expansive, simple, blocklike, and static. In the *Commercial Chemical Operations* panel, it is complex, fluid, moving, and many-layered (fig. 133). The application of paint in the *Races* panel is heavy and opaque. In the *Chemical* panel, it is fluid and transparent, demonstrating an elegance of line and the artist's mastery of watercolor technique on wet plaster. This was probably the last panel to be painted in this register and also the last panel to be designed for the entire project. As such, it is a culmination of Rivera's stylistic development on this mural project. The composition is delicately balanced between shallow foreground and deep background, between

134. *Commercial Chemical Operations*, 1932, cartoon for the south wall, charcoal on paper, 2.53 x 2.20 m. Heavy outlines define the figures, tools, and barrels, with very little shading.

135. Sketch of two chemical operation workers with color notations, 1932, graphite on paper, 15.2 x 22.9 cm.

136. Sketch of two chemical operation workers, 1932, graphite on paper, 15.2 x 22.9 cm.

137. Sketch of two chemical operation workers, 1932, graphite on paper, 15.2 x 22.9 cm. Rivera's fascination with the movements of the chemical workers is illustrated in the preliminary sketches for this panel, where the artist began to use gesture drawings. In several of these drawings, Rivera added elements to the composition, such as the figure with the torch at the lower left. Rivera's mind and hand worked so quickly that he was able to arrange the outline of the final fresco panel after having merely sketched its individual elements at the chemical plant.

138. Sketch of the design for the *Commercial Chemical Operations* panel, 1932, graphite on paper, 15.2 x 22.9 cm. Rivera organized this sketch according to the golden section. The heads of the two workers with the handle meet in the center and top third of the composition, marked by a horizontal line that runs just under the heads.

movement and stasis, and between the bulk of human figures and slim architectural elements. It is a triumph of modernism in which the composition, subject, and medium meld in perfect harmony. Had Rivera used this style throughout the project, the Detroit murals would have looked very different.[51]

North Wall *Sulfur and Potash* Panel: Below the *Chemical* panel, the natural state of sulfur and potash is shown (fig. 133). The crystals on the left are halite, or table salt; the crystals on the right are sulfur. In the center, spherical objects in four groups are suspended in gaseous fumes emanating from the salt and sulfur. McMeekin sees in this the illustration of the origin of life as proposed by Charles Darwin: "It is often said that all the conditions for the first production of a living organism are now present which could ever have been present. But if (and oh what a big if!) we could conceive of some warm little pond, with all sorts of ammonia and phosphoric salts, light, heat, electricity, etc. present so that a protein compound was chemically formed, ready to undergo still more complex changes . . . "[52] This panel continues the theme of the development of life from inanimate material. It also is directly opposite the *Cells Suffocated by Poisonous Gas* panel (fig. 120), which dramatizes the natural and spontaneous growth of life in a combination of chemicals and the destruction of life through humanity's misuse of chemicals.

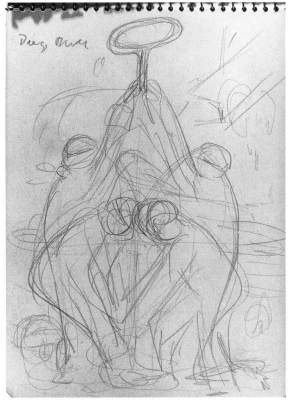

139–142. Four sketches of
chemical operation workers,
1932, graphite on paper, 15.2 x
22.9 cm. each.

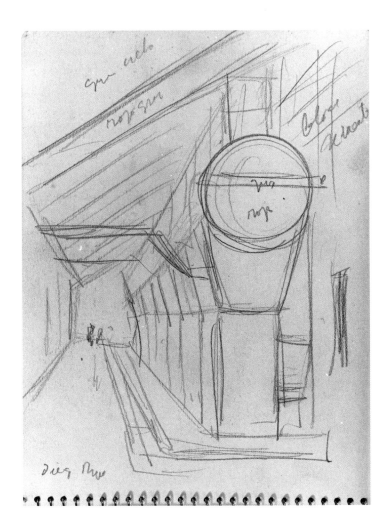

143. Sketch of a chemical vat, 1932, graphite on paper, 15.2 x 22.9 cm.

144. Sketch of chemical operations, 1932, graphite on paper, 15.2 x 22.9 cm.

145. *Production and Manufacture
of Engine and Transmission,*
detail of the north wall, fresco.

North Wall: *Production and Manufacture of Engine and Transmission*

The largest panel of the north wall, signed and dated at lower left "January 3, 1933," represents all the important operations in the production and manufacture of the interior of the automobile, specifically the engine and transmission housing of the 1932 Ford V-8 (fig. 145). One of the first stages in the production of steel is carried out in the blast furnaces, where iron ore, coke, and limestone are reduced by heat to make iron. A blast furnace that is being tapped appears in the center. The steel milling processes then continue in the predella panels below.

Rivera included a variety of faces and physiques in his figures, reflecting the multiracial work force at Ford as well as his own assistants on the mural project. E. P. Richardson's notes on the portraits indicate Rivera's intent to include many different types of people. He labeled them "Bulgarian" (Stephen Dimitroff, 7); "Texan" (Arthur Niendorf, 8); "Mexican" (9); "Canadian" (Clifford Wight, 10); "German"(11); "Yankee" (Frank Spinney [the museum gardener], 12); "Negro" (figure pushing the cart left in front of Spinney); "Japanese" (Ford engineer, 16); and "Swede" (Museum guard, 17).[53]

Rivera's emphasis on the multiracial workforce in the automobile panels expressed a Marxist hope for the future power of the working class; it was shaped by a concept of race from the early 1920s in Mexico. Great attention and value was placed on Mexican Indian culture by President Obregon's administration in an effort to bring disparate social classes together. Indians, for the first time in Mexico, were valued for their historical connection to past ancient

146–148. Three sketches of
workers, 1932, graphite on paper,
15.2 x 22.9 cm. each.

149–151. Three sketches of
workers, 1932, graphite on paper,
15.2 x 22.9 cm. each.

152. Base of blast furnace,
Charles Sheeler, photograph,
1927; 23.8 x 18.4 cm.

153. Detail, north wall automotive
panel, blast furnace, fresco.

154. Multiple spindle machine with reaming tools, Motor Assembly Plant, 1934. Electronic motor-driven multiple spindle machines ream the valve ports to the right size in the engine block.

155. Detail, north wall automotive panel, multiple spindles, fresco.

156. Foreman posing with presses, 1932.

157. Detail, showing Rivera's self-portrait in a bowler hat, north wall automotive panel, fresco.

156. Foreman posing with presses, 1932.

157. Detail, showing Rivera's self-portrait in a bowler hat, north wall automotive panel, fresco.

civilizations. In a metaphorical sense, Rivera viewed Detroit's multiracial work-force as the indigenous people of the city's industrial culture and as such its link to the civilization of the future.

Rivera combined the interiors of five buildings at the Rouge: the blast furnace, open hearth furnace, production foundry, motor assembly plant, and steel rolling mills. He combined another five buildings in the south wall automotive panel: Pressed Steel Building (now Dearborn Stamping Plant); B Building (now Dearborn Assembly Plant); Spring and Upset Building; By-Products Building; Glass Plant. Albert Kahn's designs for the Rouge had revolutionized factory architecture.

In the 1920s the Rouge plant began rapidly expanding until it was soon to become the largest industrial plant in the world. Huge factory buildings sprawled over the vast acreage, connected by a network of railroad tracks. In 1921 Kahn built the main power plant with its eight tall smokestacks, which became a familiar landmark on the horizon. Characteristic examples of the many buildings which followed were the glass plant and open hearth mills of 1924 and 1925. Here clerestories and butterfly roofs were dramatic expressions of functional requirements. The detached smoke-stacks of the glass plant achieved a monumental quality.[54]

The north and south wall automotive panels use new compositional devices Rivera drew from his cubist paintings as well as from photos and film montage. He isolated the individual manufacturing and production process and represented each in a separate perspective scheme so that one can clearly differentiate each process. He ties them together via curving conveyor lines, so that each section is visually connected to the next. The dramatic shifts in near and distant views were innovative devices that he adapted from Alexandr Rodchenko's photographs and Sergei Eisenstein's films, which he encountered in Moscow in 1928 as one of the founding members of the October Group.[55]

The blast furnace that is the dominant background image (figs. 152, 153) is the terminus of a processional way created by two rows of multiple spindles accompanied by conveyor lines. Electronic motor-driven multiple spindle machines ream the valve ports to the right size in the engine block. The valve ports are part of the intake and exhaust system of the engine. The prominence

159. Conveyor with engine parts, 1932.

160. Sketch of foundry and motor assembly operations, 1932, graphite on paper, 15.2 x 22.9 cm.

given the multiple spindles in the fresco is due not to their function but to their form. Unlike in all other representations of machines on the north and south wall automotive panels, Rivera exaggerated the actual scale of the spindle machines and magnified them to tower over the figures and dominate the panel. Two reasons may have contributed to this deviation—a need for compositional balance and Rivera's desire to point out the analogy between these machines and pre-Columbian sculpture, specifically the guardian figures at Tula (see fig. 193 for reference to Tula). Two rows of multiple spindles divide the panel and provide dominant compositional elements that echo the symmetrical division of the upper two registers on the north wall as well as the south wall. The machines can also be seen as monolithic guardian images that flank the entrance to the assembly lines, extending into deep space and giving the impression of forming an avenue, with the blast furnace at the end. The result is a harmonious compositional device that combines the illusion of deep space through the use of Renaissance perspective and a cubist/montage organization. This is a radical departure from the usual style in fresco painting, which preserved the flat plane of the wall in its composition.

The artist's self-reflection is seen in Rivera's inconspicuous self-portrait (fig. 157) on the north wall automotive panel, placing himself as an observer.

161. Gear silent test, Motor Assembly Plant, 1932.

162. Detail, north wall automotive panel, Gear silent test, fresco.

It is significant that Rivera changed the conception of himself from a worker in the San Francisco School of Fine Arts mural to an observer in Detroit where he became the visionary ambassador. Multiplicity of race is seen in the work force, where all races are drawn together into the gigantic technological systems and perform repetitive, ritual acts. Even though the reality of racial segregation existed in the "clean" and "dirty" jobs at the Rouge, all races were put to work. Rivera's figures of the four races symbolize and celebrate the diverse work force.[56]

Rivera's preliminary ideas for the automotive panels began with rectangular, iconic, and hierarchic images. The north wall automotive panel composition focused on the open hearth operations, where gigantic ladles are used to combine all the ingredients of steel, which are heated into molten metal and poured into ingot molds. Rivera created an iconic image of two workmen flanking the open hearth ladle (figs. 171–173). The workmen are so monumental in scale that they diminish the size of the actual ladle, which, in reality, is at least five times larger than the human figure. Rivera's original intent was to monumentalize the worker.

As Rivera studied the industrial processes more carefully, he abandoned the images of the iconic workers and created an integrated composition capturing

163. Sketch for the north, east, and south walls, 1932, graphite on paper, 15.2 x 22.9 cm.

164. Sketch for the north wall composition, 1932, graphite on paper, 15.2 x 22.9 cm.

165. Sketch for the north wall composition, 1932, graphite on paper, 15.2 x 22.9 cm.

166–168. Three sketches for the north wall composition with central placement of the blast furnace, 1932, graphite on paper, 15.2 x 22.9 cm. each.

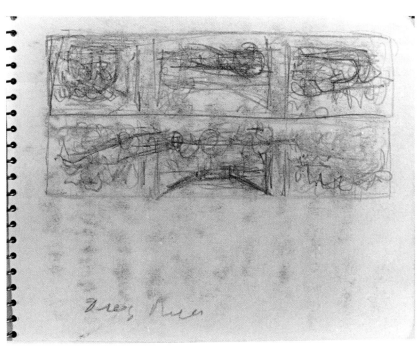

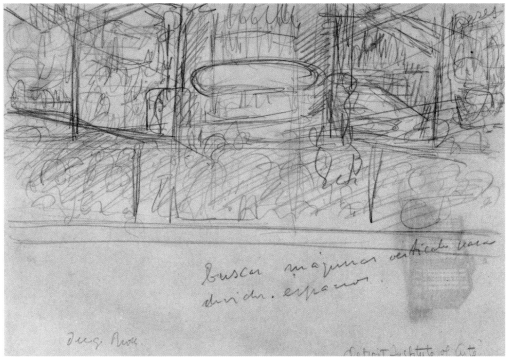

169. Sketch of three workers for the north wall automotive panel, 1932, graphite on paper, 15.2 x 22.9 cm. Rivera's preliminary idea for the north wall automotive panel was a trio of workers shaking hands, reminiscent of the representations of the worker, soldier, and farmer in the Secretaría and Chapingo murals. The composition then changes to include specific automotive processes and becomes rectangular, iconic, and hierarchic (fig. 170).

170 and 171. Two sketches for the north wall, 1932, graphite on paper, 21.6 x 27.9 cm. each.

172–174. Three sketches for the north wall automotive panel, 1932, ink on paper, 21.6 x 27.9 cm. each.

Diego Rivera

Study for [illegible]

Detroit Institute of Art

Diego Rivera

175. Sketch for the north wall composition, 1932, graphite on paper, 15.2 x 22.9 cm.

176. *Theme=Rectangles D'Or,* sketch for the north wall composition to determine golden section, 1932, graphite on paper, 21.6 x 27.9 cm.

177. Two sketches for the north wall automotive panel, 1932, watercolor, ink, and graphite on paper, 21.6 x 27.9 cm. each

the movement of conveyors, workers, and machines. This transformation from static to dynamic can be seen in his sketches. In the upper right center of the second sketch, the monumental figure of the worker turning a gauge wheel appears again (fig. 175). Rivera was not only searching for the appropriate images for the north wall automotive panel; he was also experimenting with the composition. When he changed the central image from the open hearth ladle to the blast furnace, the composition surrounding it became organized in cubistic style. The rectangular "windows" give way to a more angular or refracted organization of space. The preliminary sketches illustrate how the iconic figures of monumental workers diminished in scale and the composition became more identifiable and fluid.

The only known color sketches for the Detroit murals are two watercolors of the north wall automotive panel, in which Rivera completely breaks away from the rectangular "windows" to create a more open, flowing composition that implies movement, not only of the workers but of the industrial processes themselves, through the use of sinuous, snakelike conveyors (fig. 177).

The images generally refer to the blast furnace, open hearth furnace, and

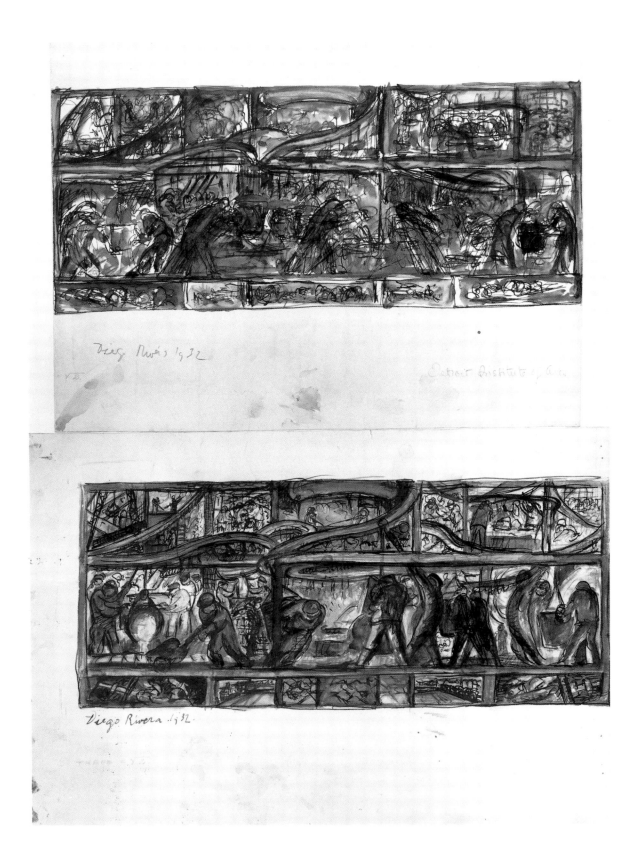

Diego Rivera 1932

Detroit Institute of Arts

Diego Rivera 1932

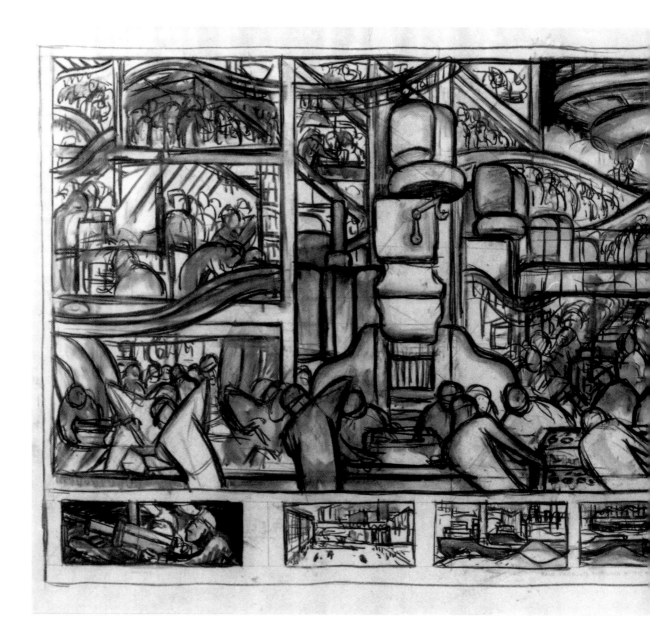

178. *Production and Manufacture of Engine and Transmission*, sketch for the north wall automotive panel, 1932, charcoal on paper, 45.7 x 83.8 cm. Rivera originally included mining and Great Lakes shipping scenes as a continuous series of predella panels.

foundry, all operational elements necessary in the making of steel. The compositions are divided along three horizontal registers. The top register in each watercolor places the blast furnace at the center, with related operations in rectangular spaces on either side. The middle registers depict aspects of pouring molten metal into engine block molds. And the lowest register of the second sketch depicts mining operations. Bringing mining, blast furnace, and foundry operations together led Rivera to a greater understanding of relationships among these processes.

The lack of color sketches and the harmonious color relationships between the four walls attest to Rivera's consummate color sense. Davis recalled that Rivera only had an initial concern about color relationships when he began the fresco process. This was the reason Rivera asked him to touch up some areas on the north wall races panel and the automotive panel (fire of the blast furnace) with casein paint. As mentioned earlier, as the pigment dries into the wet plaster the colors change slightly in intensity. It was imperative that adjacent sections be painted as close in time as possible so that colors matched. Rivera's color scheme is one of the elements that unites all four walls of fresco so that they can be read as a whole. The upper registers and upper levels of the lower panels are more saturated with opaque color. The color diminishes as one reads down the panels to the monchrome gray panels at the lower edge of the north and

Diego Rivera. 1932

south walls. Thus, the farther away the panels are from the viewer, the more intense the color. Rivera used the white plaster as a watercolorist uses the natural color of the paper. His use of the ground as color is most evident in the rendering of the machines where the shine of the metal is conveyed by letting the unpainted plaster appear as highlights. The most opaque areas are the deep cobalt blue skies in the races panels.

Since there is no longer a cloth awning draped over the wooden beams, sunlight shines directly in through the skylight on the north and west walls. On cloudy days when sunlight dramatically appears and disappears the fresco colors are naturally spotlit with quick bursts of animated light. Every day the colors change and values heighten or deepen with changing weather conditions. Rivera experienced these daily and seasonal light changes and had to compensate by maintaining a mental image of the color scheme as he painted through the summer, fall, and winter of 1932–1933.

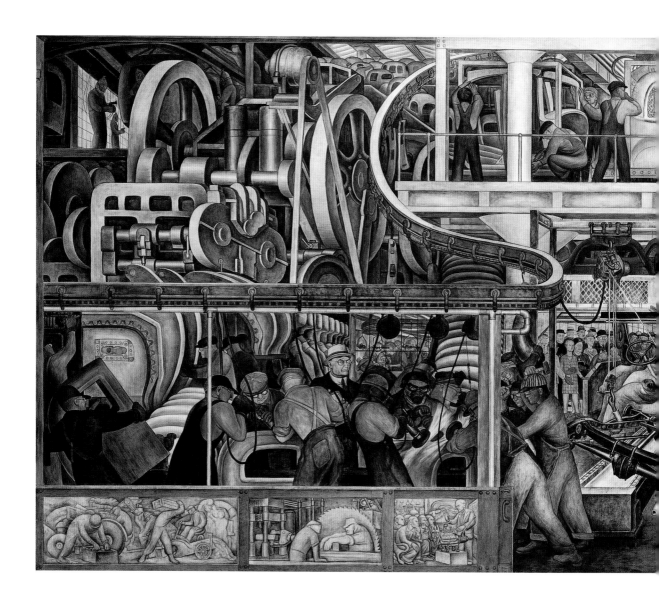

179. *Production of Automobile Exterior and Final Assembly,* the south wall automotive panel, fresco.

South Wall: *Production of Automobile Exterior and Final Assembly*

The major panel of the south wall is devoted to the production of the exterior of the 1932 Ford V-8 (fig. 179) and its final assembly. Unlike the north wall, this panel is not organized in production sequence, although all the major operations are included. The creation of the automobile body parts begins at the right, where the monumental stamping press produces fenders out of large sheets of steel. A cluster of stamping presses appears in the upper left section. The stamping press was based on an outdated model which Rivera would have seen only in photographic form (fig. 180), since the 1932 model had the internal mechanisms sheathed (fig. 181). The earlier stamping press makes a closer visual comparison to the monumental Aztec creator deity Coatlicue (fig. 185). This visual comparison is important to Rivera's interpretation of modern industry, as discussed in the next chapter.

After the body parts are stamped into forms, they are spot welded. Spot welding is carried out to the lower left of the stamping press. The surface is then smoothed out in the buffing process, which is in the lower left foreground. Workmen are being observed by a foreman in hat and glasses. The features of the foreman are based on those of Mead L. Bricker, an important Ford production manager who was notorious for speeding up the assembly line (figs. 196–199).[57]

At the top of the panel in the center is the welding buck where the separate parts are welded into the body of the car. To the right of the buck, women sew upholstery, and to the left, painters spray the bodies before they are conveyed

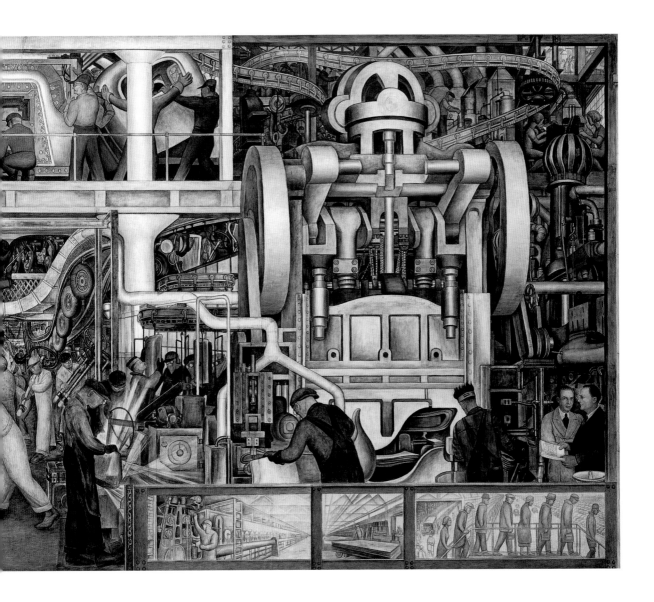

into the ovens. Below the welding buck is the final assembly of the car. Men use pullies to secure the chassis to the line. Along the line, the motors are lowered onto the chassis, wheels attached, and the body secured. At the very end of the assembly line Rivera painted a tiny red car speeding off into time and space. Rivera was less interested in the product than in the process of automobile production.

Two groups of people are not working in this panel. The first group is a tour group made up of sour-faced bourgeoisie (fig. 200). At Pablo Davis's suggestion, Rivera drew upon comic strip characters like Dick Tracy and the Katzenjammer Kids as models for this group. He included a priest and a dour matron with a Christian cross around her neck. In all the criticisms leveled at the murals by Catholic and Episcopal priests, no one recognized Rivera's caricature of them in this panel.

The other two people who are observers are standing at the lower right section. Rivera painted these two figures in the traditional position of Italian Renaissance donors. On the left is a portrait of Edsel B. Ford and on the right a portrait of William Valentiner (fig. 201). Valentiner holds a dedication paper of the mural project (see page 35 and fig. 42).

Judging from the number of sketches alone, Rivera was fascinated with the stamping presses he saw at the Rouge. All of his sketches show the 1932 model of the presses where the internal mechanisms are sheathed with plates of steel. Some sketches (figs. 183 and 184) are careful renderings where the artist

180. Stamping press, 1927.

181. Stamping press, 1932.

182. Sketch of a workman at a stamping press, 1932, charcoal on paper, 15.2 x 22.9 cm.

183 and 184. Two sketches of stamping presses, 1932, graphite on paper, 15.2 x 22.9 cm. each.

became familiar with the shape and function of the machines and their relative size to the workers. Others anthropomorphize the presses where the flywheels become arm-like appendages and the tops are given faces (fig. 182). Ultimately, the press in the fresco took on the form of Coatlicue (fig. 185). And in order to better portray that Aztec deity he painted an outdated press from a 1927 photograph taken by Charles Sheeler (fig. 180). Sheeler had been hired by the Ford Motor Company to document the machines and factories at the Rouge that appeared in the company's publications and promotions. A photomontage mural by Sheeler that featured the stamping press was included in the exhibition "Murals by American Painters and Photographers" at the Museum of Modern Art in 1932. Rivera probably saw this exhibition when he visited New York to negotiate with Abby Aldrich Rockefeller and her son Nelson to paint at Rockefeller Center.

185. *Coatlicue*, Aztec goddess of creation and war, stone, h. 3.5 m. Rivera saw the stamping press and its function as parallel to the cosmic function of Coatlicue, who through her tremendous power creates humanity and in return demands human sacrifice to maintain universal order.

186. Detail, stamping press and spot welder, fresco. Rivera used an old-style press in which the "skeleton" is more apparent, making the machine more dramatically anthropormorphic.

187. Spot welders, 1932.

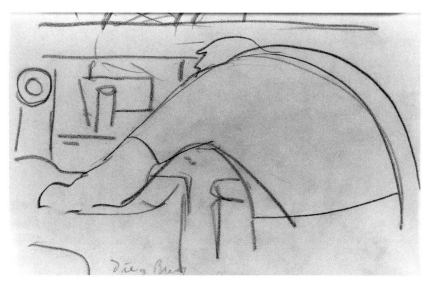

188. Workman with hair blown by the stamping press, 1932, graphite on paper, 15.2 x 22.9 cm.

189. Workman at a stamping press, 1932, graphite on paper, 1932, 15.2 x 22.9 cm.

Rivera heavily relied on the use of photographs for many mural passages even when he had made many sketches of the same machines or workers. The spot welder who appears in front of the stamping press is taken from a posed photograph by a Ford photographer (fig. 181). The photograph was taken at a time when no other workers were in the factory. The final fresco image of the worker shows him in overalls with his cap reversed and wearing gloves. Rivera properly outfitted him to work in the fresco. The posed men in the photograph appear unaccustomed to welding and protect their hands from the grease of the fenders by using paper towels (fig. 187).

190. Beginning of final assembly of the Ford V-8, B Building, 1932.

191. Detail, south wall automotive panel, final assembly, fresco.

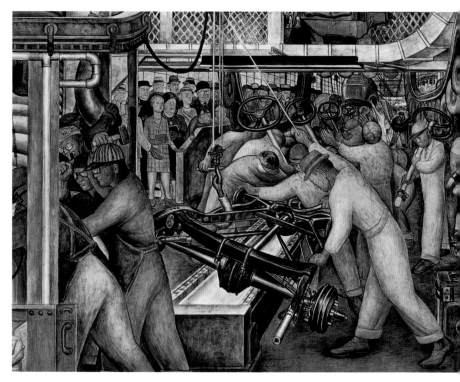

The photograph of final assembly shows the reality of the sparse workforce at the Rouge (fig. 190). Where Rivera's murals teem with workers down the final assembly line (fig. 191), the actual line employed very few men. Again, Rivera changed the clothing from a smock to overalls. What is accurate, however, is every detail of the chasis, the pulley system, and the conveyor line.

192. Sketch of final assembly of the Ford V-8, 1932, graphite on paper, 15.2 x 22.9 cm.

193. Sketch of final assembly of the Ford V-8, 1932, graphite on paper, 15.2 x 22.9 cm., with the inscription "*para el obrero/H control/sacrificio a Tullan*" (for the worker/check point/sacrifice at Tula). The inscription refers to the ancient archeological edifice of Tula north of Mexico City. Rivera drew analogies between the industrial process at the Rouge and the ancient sacrificial sites in Mexico.

194. Sketch of automobile body welders, 1932, graphite on paper, 15.2 x 22.9 cm.

195. Sketch of final assembly of the Ford V-8, 1932, graphite on paper, 15.2 x 22.9 cm.

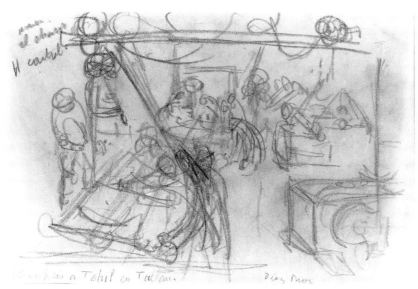

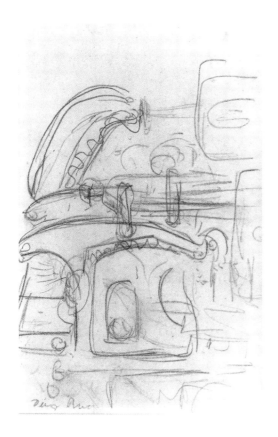

196. Mead L. Bricker, Charles Sorenson, and unidentified figure at Willow Run Bomber Plant, 1942. The foreman figure on the lower left of the south wall automotive panel was once believed to be a generalized portrait of Charles E. Sorenson, who was responsible for the mechanically actuated assembly line that revolutionized the automobile industry. But it is more likely a portrait of Mead L. Bricker, another important Ford production manager at that time who was notorious for speeding up the assembly line.

197. Sketch of foreman with two workers, 1932, graphite on paper, 15.2 x 22.9 cm.

198. Detail of south wall automotive panel, fresco. A foreman in hat and glasses supervises this operation. This figure represents the constant hostile supervision at Ford by production managers who were more interested in quotas than in the conditions of the workers or their environment. Large conveyors at the lower left carry body parts to the next operation—bumping and grinding.

199. Sketch of Mead L. Bricker, 1932, graphite on paper, 15.2 x 22.9 cm.

200. Detail of spectators looking at final assembly in the south wall automotive panel, fresco. Rivera's bourgeoisie are dour, well-fed figures who look blankly or disapprovingly at the workers. The tour guide, in a suit and hat, has his back to the viewer and gestures toward the assembly line with his right hand. A priest and two devout ladies adorned with crosses prominently head the tour group, while two boys wearing beanies crawl over the gate to get a better view. Some figures are reminiscent of comic strip characters such as Dick Tracy and the Katzenjammer Kids. Rivera was a great fan of the comics and may have had them in mind.

201. Detail of portraits of William Valentiner and Edsel B. Ford in the south wall automotive panel, fresco. The portrait of Ford was based on an official Ford Motor Company photograph. The portrait of Valentiner captures the intensity of the director's character in his strong but delicate features, but these are diminished by the oversized body, which was not taken from a life study. Valentiner holds the dedicatory text in his hand (see page 35).

202. Sketch of an upholstery worker, 1932, graphite on paper, 15.2 x 22.9 cm.

Women rarely appear as workers in the fresco, primarily because they were restricted to "light" work such as assembly of small parts and sewing upholstery. It was not until a brief period during World War II when male workers were at the front that women were hired to do heavy assembly jobs at the Rouge. Rivera's sketches show women at work dressed in coveralls with protective caps and goggles (figs. 202–206). They are portrayed with the same seriousness and concentration given to male workers. Lucienne Bloch recalled that when it came to work Rivera expected the same abilities and energies from both genders.

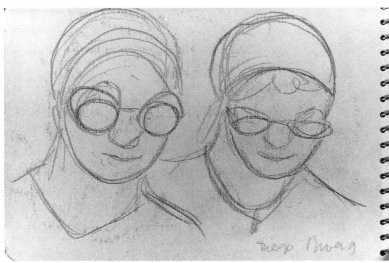

203–205. Three sketches of upholstery workers, 1932, graphite on paper, 15.2 x 22.9 cm. each.

206. Detail of upholstery workers on the south wall automotive panel, fresco. Sewing upholstery was one of the few jobs women were hired to do at the Rouge.

151

207. Sketches for the south wall automotive panel, 1932, graphite on paper.

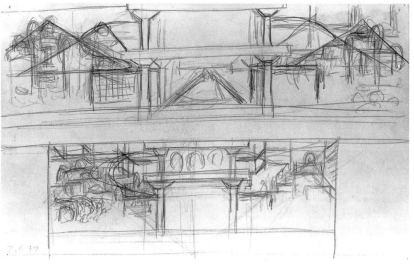

The south wall composition was given greater stability than the flowing north wall because of the size of the stamping press and the placement of the welding buck on pylons over final assembly. Rivera altered the composition in the fresco and gave it more fluidity by setting the assembly off at an angle and emphasizing the conveyors that weave the foreground and background together. The predella panels in the presentation drawing depict foundry and milling operations. This would have followed the mining and shipping in production sequence from the north wall predellas. The predellas were originally conceived as a continuous band across the lower edge of the panel, but this composition blocked visual access to the workers and factories beyond (fig. 208).

208. *Manufacture of Automobile Exterior and Final Assembly*, 1932, sketch for the south wall automotive panel, charcoal on paper, 45.7 x 83.8 cm. Rivera greatly altered the stamping presses in the fresco for the south wall automotive panel. In this sketch Rivera used the newer model, in which most of the press is swathed in steel.

209. Detail, north wall predella panel, open hearth operations: workers punch in at the time clock, fresco.

Predella Panels

Apart from their aforementioned similarity to Italian medieval and Renaissance altar paintings, Rivera's predella panels are also reminiscent, in their monochromaticism, of traditional grisaille paintings, where the intent was to create the illusion of a sculptural frieze. Rivera had studied grisaille paintings in Paris. These small panels also recall Mexican ex voto paintings, where major religious figures appear at the top, the event being commemorated is in the center, and the description appears below. He used the predella both to show a day in the life of a worker and to illustrate some of the major production processes not easily included in the larger panels. The predella panels appear as if fixed to steel gates, which separate the viewer from the workers in the automotive panel. The center of each gate is open (note the handles and chains on each sliding door), inviting the viewer into the factory space.

The predella panels and preparatory sketches are illustrated here in order from left to right, on the north wall (figs. 209–224) and on the south wall (figs. 225–235).

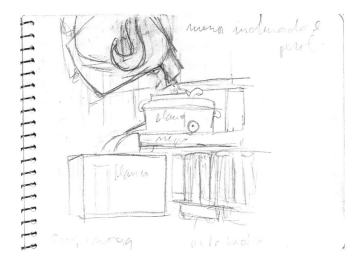

210. Detail, north wall predella panel, open hearth operations: ingots in the foreground and molten metal being poured into ingot molds, fresco.

211. Sketch of a pour at the open hearth furnace, 1932, graphite on paper, 15.2 x 22.9 cm.

212. Sketch of a pour at the open hearth furnace, 1932, graphite on paper, 15.2 x 22.9 cm., with the inscription "*menor inclinado el perol/blanco/negro/blanco*" (small tilted pot/white/black/white).

213. Sketch of men, machine (?) pouring molten metal into ingot molds, 1932, graphite on paper, 15.2 x 22.9 cm.

214. Detail, north wall predella panel, Rolling Mill: ingots being transferred by buggy to furnaces for reheating before rolling, fresco.

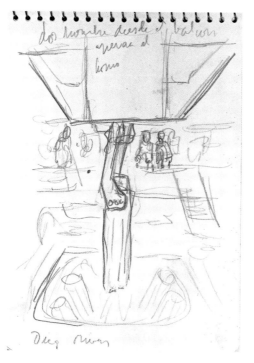

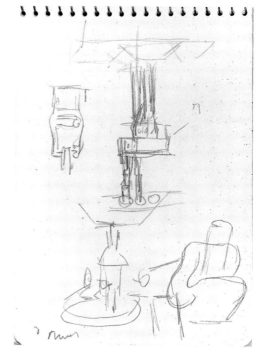

215. Sketch of crane moving ingots, 1932, graphite on paper, 15.2 x 22.9 cm., with the inscription "*los dos hombres desde el balcon operan el horno*" (two men from the balcony operate the oven).

216. Sketch of ingot operations, 1932, graphite on paper, 15.2 x 22.9 cm.

217. Sketch of ingot buggy, 1932, graphite on paper, 15.2 x 22.9 cm., with the inscription "*hay dos serpientes traga fierros entre cuatro hornos*" (there are two serpents swallowing iron between four ovens). The inscription refers to the ingot buggies as serpent mouths swallowing the ingots.

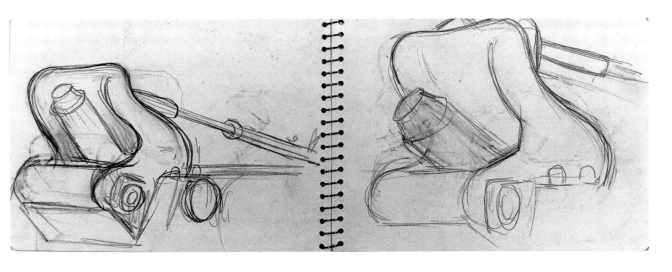

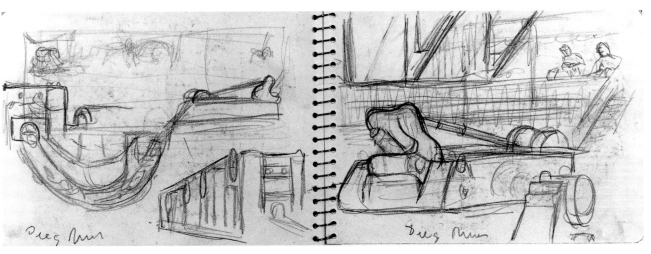

218. Two sketches of ingot buggies, 1932, graphite on paper,
15.2 x 22.9 cm. each.

219. Two sketches of milling
processes, 1932, graphite on
paper, 15.2 x 22.9 cm. each.

220. Detail, north wall predella panel, Billet Mill: ingots being rolled into bars, fresco.

221. Detail, north wall predella panel, Bar Mill: metal bars being piled and cut, fresco.

222. Detail, north wall predella panel, Tandem Mill: workers taking a lunch break, fresco.

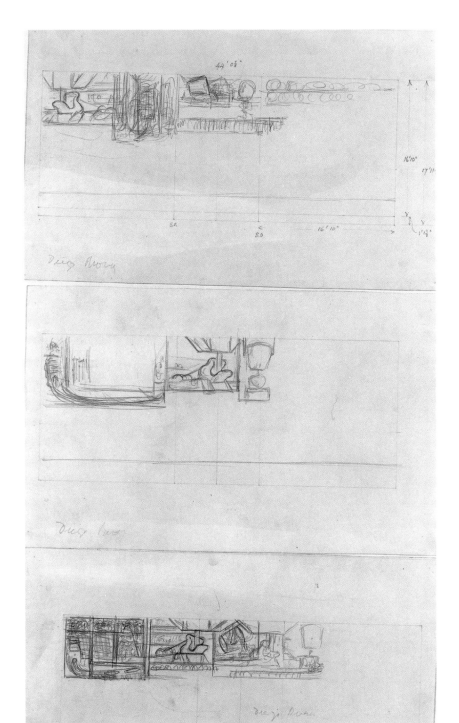

223. Three sketches of milling operations for the north wall automotive panel, 1932, graphite on paper 15.2 x 22.9 cm. each.

224. Sketch of the billet mill operations, 1932, graphite on paper, 15.2 x 22.9 cm.

225. Detail, south wall predella panel, By-Products Building: by-products of the coke ovens being made into fertilizer, fresco.

226. Detail, south wall predella panel, Spring and Upset Building: making parts to repair machines, fresco.

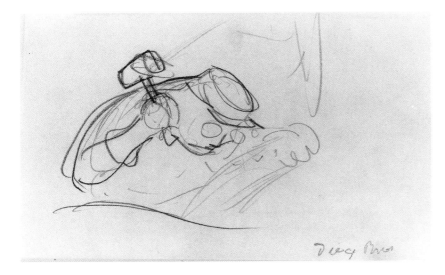

227–229. Three sketches for the south wall predella panel of repairs in Spring and Upset Building, 1932, graphite on paper, 15.2 x 22.9 cm. each.

230. Detail, south wall predella panel, B Building: trade school engine class led by Henry Ford, fresco. The trade school panel depicts Henry Ford as an instructor, although he was never actually a teacher. Ford is holding forth with his right hand raised and index finger pointing above him. His right hand is surrounded by figures in the background seated with heads bent over books at a long library table, giving the impression that they are bowing to Ford's hand.

Ford is lecturing about the V-8 engine, on display in the foreground of the panel. Rivera transformed the engine into a mechanical dog by altering its head and adding two metal ears and a tongue flapping down from the mouth. The image is reminiscent of a Mexican hairless breed of dog that appears as an object of veneration in pre-conquest pottery and was a source of food for the Aztecs. Dogs of this breed exist today as pets in Mexico. Here the engine is Ford's faithful doglike companion.

The pose of the students is reminiscent of Auguste Rodin's *The Thinker*. A cast of *The Thinker* was on display in the Great Hall adjacent to the Garden Court when the new museum opened in 1927 (fig. 67).

231 and 232. Two sketches of motors on a conveyor at the Motor Assembly Plant, 1932, graphite on paper, 15.2 x 22.9 cm. each.

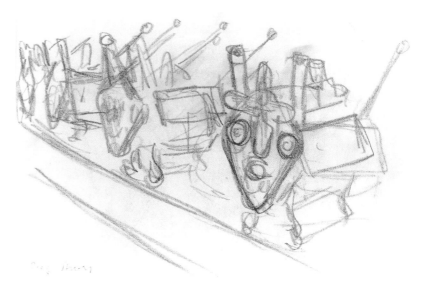

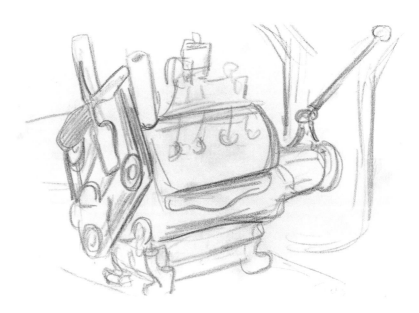

233. Detail, south wall predella panel, Glass Plant: rolling operations, fresco.

234. Detail, south wall predella panel, Glass Plant: polishing and stacking operations, fresco.

235. Detail of the final predella panel on the south wall, fresco. Workers line up to receive their pay at an armored truck in the Production Foundry (depicted as the Motor Assembly Plant) and cross the pedestrian bridge above Miller Road. Rivera would have actually seen very few cars parked in the lots as the work force had been drastically reduced during the Depression. He chose, however, to suggest the Rouge at the height of its productivity.

236. Diagram of production and manufacturing processes at the Rouge, 1932, This diagram of clippings pasted on paper glued to cardboard was probably assembled by a Ford engineer to help Rivera understand the relationships between the production and manufacturing processes at the Rouge.

Rivera's interpretation of Detroit industry was based, as we have seen, on his world view, which included ancient and contemporary religious traditions, Marxist political ideals, pan-American cultural nationalism, Fordism and industrial determinism, and seemingly disparate artistic traditions—ancient and contemporary Mexican religious imagery and popular art; iconography, moral didacticism, and fresco technique derived from the Italian Renaissance; an academic organization of the picture plane according to the golden section; a cubist and Russian avant-garde use of space and proportion; a modern classical figural style; and a futurist depiction of movement. We will see that by analyzing the creative process of the fresco cycle it becomes evident that Rivera's understanding of the manufacturing and production processes at the Rouge corresponded to the development of an artistic theme that infused modern technology with meaning from an ancient Mexican context. The idea of a cultural continuum that extended from Mexico's ancient past to its present, and which was so important to the emergence of a new national Mexican identity after the revolution, also informed the mural cycle in Detroit.

After the Mexican Revolution, cultural nationalism was introduced as a means of creating public consciousness about the value of indigenous culture. Projects like the Mexican Mural Movement as well as educational reform were meant to bridge gaping economic, racial, and social divides. Rivera, brought up by both a mother who was a devout Catholic and a nurse devoted to religion in the form of ancient Mexican beliefs, regaled the café crowd in Paris as a young artist with tales of ancient sacrifices. But he also took time to study ancient Aztec codices in Spanish libraries and archives. Those commissioned just after the conquest by Catholic monks from *tlacuilos* (native scribes) provided Rivera's generation with a wealth of information on ancient religious practices.

One of the first collectors of ancient Mexican sculpture, Rivera, as mentioned earlier, would eventually build Anahuacalli to house his art works. Mexican archeology was in its early phase during his lifetime. He was familiar with the major archeological sites, such as Tula and Teotihuacán, near Mexico City, and those in Oaxaca, Chiapas, and Guatemala.

Rivera's first exposure to a major industrial complex was at the Ford Motor Company's Rouge plant. Its sheer energy, power, and magnitude made him associate it with the vast archeological sites in Mexico, and the individual industrial processes became analogous to religious rituals.

He made explicit references to ancient Mexican sculpture and archeological sites in his sketches. For example, a sketch of the ingots being transported between ovens in gigantic metal buggies has the note *"hay dos serpientes traga fierros entre cuatro hornos"* (there are two serpents swallowing iron between four ovens) (see fig. 217). Rivera mentally anthropomorphized the buggies into the serpent god Quetzalcoatl. And on a sketch of the assembly line he wrote, *"Para el obrero/ H Control/ Sacrificio a Tohil en Tullan"* (For the worker/check point/ sacrifice at Tohil in Tula). He also made an explicit analogy between the stamping presses and the Aztec creation deity Coatlicue (see fig. 185).

These notes were disparate thoughts until Rivera began to understand how the industrial processes fit together. There is a definable moment when the Rouge, for him, became associated with human sacrifice, and the four walls of the court became the set for this ancient ritual. It was this moment that prompted him to develop a scheme for all twenty-seven panels of the court, lent thematic coherence to the entire cycle, and prompted a dramatic change in his mural style from one that was strictly hierachical to that of a dynamically flowing composition.

The key to Rivera's understanding and interpretation of the Rouge is found in a diagram consisting of photographs and printed reproductions of essential industrial processes at the Rouge that were clipped from *Ford News*, the in-house publication of the Ford Motor Company (fig. 236). This diagram unlocked the Rouge for Rivera in a way that sketching in the plants or working from photographs could not. Rivera was able to understand as a whole the individual processes he had experienced in separate parts at the Rouge. He could see how raw materials follow two major paths, one to create the motor and the other the body of the car. And he was able to see the realization of Henry Ford's dream, where in one industrial complex, raw materials are transformed into automobiles by workers, energy, and machines. The diagram also helped Rivera make the philosophical leap to the meaning of technology on a large scale.

The stamping presses at the Rouge held special fascination for him (figs. 180–181). Workmen feed flat sheets of metal into the die jaws of the press and jump back when it slams down with tons of pressure to form large three-dimensional body parts. Rivera made an analogy between the sculptural forms and functions of modern machines and ancient American sculpture. The stamping press on the south wall resembles the monumental sculpture of the creation deity Coatlicue, which was originally found in Mexico City in 1790 at the site of Tenochtitlán, the Aztec capital destroyed by the Spaniards.[1] The monstrous image of Coatlicue, eight-and-a-half-feet high, was so terrifying that it was reburied for many years (see fig. 185).

Rivera greatly enlarged the vent at the top of the stamping press to give a "head" to the image. The fly wheels are broadened to echo Coatlicue's serpent arms. And Coatlicue's skin of flayed human flesh is the steel casing surrounding the "torso" of the press. Rivera's understanding of ancient religious concepts included the idea of a compact between Aztec Indians and their gods. Humans were created by the sacrifice of the gods and therefore humanity must reciprocate by sacrificing lives in order to nourish the gods with human hearts and blood. Just as the Aztecs were human fodder for the sun, Rivera drew the analogy to the factory workers who sacrifice their energy for the technological universe. In the *Detroit Industry* frescoes, the workers are analogous to the Indians and the Rouge industrial complex is analogous to the Aztec cosmos. In order to make the reference to the Aztec sculpture more apparent, Rivera deliberately used an obsolete model of a stamping press in the fresco, not one of those he sketched at the Rouge (figs. 182–184).[2] Six years later Rivera made the analogy between the stamping press and Coatlicue explicit in the major image of this mural *Pan-American Unity: The Marriage of the Artistic Expression of the North and South of this Continent* painted in 1939–1940 at the Golden Gate Exposition in San Francisco.

Narrative Sequence and Hierarchy

Marilyn Lavin has proposed a method for understanding the placement of Italian medieval and Renaissance fresco narratives in their architectural settings. She believes that frescoes on separate walls must be considered together as complete entities in order to decipher the underlying thematic programs dictated by patrons, clergymen, and artists.[3] Using Lavin's principles of analysis, the disposition of the distinct narratives of the Detroit murals becomes evident. Rivera had several stories to tell simultaneously, and each one follows a different path around, down, and across the court.

The simpler of the narratives can be read by following the registers from the top to the bottom of each wall. But to follow the more complex narrative of the sacrifice of human life for technological and cosmic order, the eye must cross the court to opposite walls and rebound to read the whole story.

On the east wall (fig. 69), there is an obvious relationship between the fertility figures of the Americas in the top register and the still lifes of fruit and vegetables below them. On the west wall (fig. 82), the descending vertical pattern presents the productive and destructive uses of technology. Below the passenger and war planes, Rivera makes his theme explicit by depicting the peaceful dove and aggressive hawk. Continuing down, the creation of the raw energy of steam relates to the hawk and the war plane, and the transformation of that energy into electricity corresponds to the dove and the passenger plane. Just as the manual labor of the worker relates to the raw power of steam, the intellectual power of the engineer/inventor relates to the transformed energy of electricity. The corner panels of the north and south walls also read down: the *Vaccination* panel relates to the *Healthy Human Embryo* below it; the gas bomb panel relates to the microscopic view of suffocating cells; the *Pharmaceutics* panel to the one showing animal surgery; and the *Commercial Chemical Operations* to the raw materials.

The states of humanity develop in a descending line from the iconic, androgynous images of the four races to the individualized portraits of workers in the automotive panels and down to the anonymous figures in the predella panels. Rivera presents humanity in three states: monumental and idealized, individual and particular, and as an anonymous mass of workers. The three states are critical to his interpretation of the role of humanity in industrial technology. The workers in the four races have specific characteristics linked, as we have seen, to the qualities of raw materials. These qualities are essential to the overall character of humanity and to a strong work force. The individual worker makes up a part of that ideal. Only through collective work on the assembly line, which Rivera saw as Henry Ford's contribution to the advancement of a socialist society, can individuals become greater than themselves and produce on a vast scale. The assembly line also produces people who have given up their individuality to the machines and industries they operate. This is made clear in the portions of the predella panels where workers appear as identical figures in rows.

For the development of technology, the viewer begins on the east wall with the early earthbound technology of agriculture (fig. 69); moves across the court to technology of the air on the west wall (fig. 82); down the west wall to the generation of electricity in the Rouge Power House #1; and then catty-corner to the central image of the blast furnace (fig. 107). Automobile technology is presented as the most modern, complex, and sophisticated of technologies. The notion of the evolution of industrial technology culminating in the creation of the automobile was first introduced to Rivera at the Henry Ford Museum. When Rivera toured the museum alone for almost a full day and a full night, he arrived at a thorough understanding of the message Ford presented there. Mechanical engineering evolved from simple to complex processes and culminated in the automobile industry, a gigantic technological system whose powers went beyond the control of workers, managers, or owners. To Ford and also to Rivera, industry was a palpable entity with a cosmic power greater than the sum of its parts.

The automotive processes form narrative patterns that loop back and forth on the north and south wall automotive panels. The cross-court pattern places the viewer in the midst of the evolution of technology; the viewer, like the artist, is all-seeing, unlike the individual personifications of the four races, whose characteristics form separate parts of humanity.

The Transfer of Energy

Rivera also tells the "story" of the transfer of energy from raw materials into machines of great power through human strength and ingenuity. The process of transforming raw materials into finished automobiles begins in the middle register of the east wall, with the geological strata of iron ore, limestone, coal, and sand depicted as the sustenance of the child in the bulb of the plant (fig. 73). The paths then split in two along the middle registers and around the north and south walls of the court, where the materials are enlarged and their properties lent to the characters of the races above. In the middle register of the west wall panel, these materials are transported by ship to the industrial port on the left (fig. 90). The raw materials are then transformed by the steam ovens in the west wall and the blast furnace in the north wall. The blast furnace is placed directly below the volcano, a symbol of primordial power (fig. 107). In the twentieth century, the volcano's spiritual meaning was updated to theosophical significance by Mexican artists such as Dr. Atl (the pseudonym of Gerardo Murillo), one of Rivera's mentors, who saw volcanoes as a source of great power that could be tapped by humans venturing up to their cones. The volcano also represents raw violence in Mariano Azuela's novel *The Underdogs*, praised as the novel of the revolution and published in book form (after its serial publication in a Mexican newspaper) three years before Rivera painted in Detroit. Rivera uses the volcano to represent the violent energy of the races and industry. The volcano is also, as discussed earlier, the symbolic natural equivalent of the pyramid, which is directly across from it on the south wall.

The volcano, as we have seen, is surrounded by hands grasping the raw materials of the earth, representing mining. The empty hands surrounding the pyramid are emblematic of the human power of struggle and sacrifice, and recall the symbolic function and ritual human sacrifice enacted at ancient Mesoamerican pyramid sites. The generalized representation of the four races as Chac Mool figures also corresponds to the function of the pyramid, turning sacrificial human hearts into sustenance for the goddess Coatlicue, who in turn transforms that energy into cosmic order and well-being.

At the north wall blast furnace, the viewer's eye is guided along a path made up of multiple spindles and workers in front of conveyors that move from the background to the foreground. The workers are bent over the conveyors as if in supplication to the spindles, whose form has been compared to the ancient guardian figures at Tula. These are the human hearts that are sacrificed on the assembly line in this technological system.

This path is connected symbolically across the court to the pyramid on the south wall panel, then vertically down to the background, where a tiny red automobile moves off the end of the assembly line (fig. 237). The scale and size of the little red car—it is only about four inches long—indicates its insignificance in the system. The assembled car is not the end point in Rivera's scheme. He depicts a circular system in which creativity (the production of automobiles, airplanes, chemicals, vaccines, and weapons) is balanced by destruction (the workers' and engineers' sacrifice of human energy) and the transformation of natural resources (iron ore, coal, sand, and limestone).

A Golden Age

Rivera reconciled the concept of modern industrial processes with ancient beliefs at a time in Detroit's history when industrial systems had failed the worker. The Depression created an atmosphere of self-doubt, fear of the future, and blame of the industrialists. The *Detroit Industry* murals present a modern

237. Detail of red car at end of final assembly in the south wall automotive panel, fresco. Rivera's cubistic and Renaissance compositional devices are employed here. He pierces the center of the panel, creating an illusion of great depth along the assembly line to the point where the tiny red car (about 10 cm.) is driven away. The surrounding composition is also arranged with multiple perspectives. Conveyors are used as framing and linking motifs. The welding buck acts as the central image, but it is not visually as weighty an image as the blast furnace, its counterpart on the north wall. The dominant image on the south wall is the formidable stamping press, which visually competes with the welding buck.

golden age, before the 1929 stock market crash, when industrial productivity, employment, and wages were at their height and Detroit was a boom town. Rivera created a nostalgia for a culture of work and labor in the automotive industry that had been radically transformed by the Depression, which created a climate where industrialists were despised as being reckless capitalists who abdicated moral economy. Moral economy holds that industrialists have an obligation to control the production, manufacture, and sale of commodities in order to protect the interests of the community of consumers. Moral economy was bankrupt in 1932–1933 Detroit.

While the ancient contextual meaning of the murals may not have been evident to viewers in 1933, the concept of a golden age of technology was not lost on either the industrialists or the workers. Through the ritual of work, these murals provided hope in a world that had collapsed around workers and managers. Through the *Detroit Industry* fresco, workers and industrialists could share a nostalgia for a work environment that had radically changed. The artist located the image of industry in a fictitious past that sustained the power of the benevolent industrialist and the devoted laborer.

The murals also invoke the communist concept of assimilation of culture. Marx and Lenin advocated using the culture of the dominant classes to create a new national culture for the proletariat by extracting and reinterpreting democratic or socialistic elements of existing cultures.[4] Giving new meaning to seemingly disparate forms, such as the nativity from Renaissance paintings, on the one hand, and pre-conquest codices, on the other, is within the procedures recommended by Marx and Lenin to reach the masses with recognizable forms and lead them into the future. "The new art will revive all the old forms, which arose in the course of the development of the creative spirit. The disintegration and decline of these forms are not absolute, that is they do not mean that these forms are absolutely incompatible with the spirit of the new age. All that is necessary is for the poet of the new epoch to re-think in a new way the thoughts of mankind, and to re-feel its feelings."[5]

While Rivera espoused a communist world view, the traditional Marxian interpretation of the *Detroit Industry* murals referred to in the Introduction so narrowly defines the fresco cycle as to render it meaningless as a modern aesthetic object that reflects the history and circumstances of the city and the intent of the artist. Wood, Smith, and Craven focus on Taylorism, the theory of scientific management proposed by Frederick Winslow Taylor at the turn of the century that led to the assembly line. When Taylorism, in the form of mechanized robot-like workers on pristine assembly lines, was not found in the *Detroit Industry* murals, then the cycle was called an anomaly. Wood was particularly at a loss:

> . . . what was realist or "proletarian" about an art that depicted clean and well-fed workers in apparent harmony with management as well as with the latest technology, producing cars they could scarcely afford, in a plant where production was down to one-fifth of 1929 levels and that only a few weeks before Rivera's arrival had been the target of a 3,000-strong Communist-organized hunger march that ended at the factory gates in the shooting of three workers [five workers] and injury to a score of others?[6]

It is difficult to see the murals through the lens of one political ideology because Rivera's ideology was not singular in scope. Just as he drew upon many artistic styles to create his mural style, he also drew on many ideologies and synthesized them into a coherent whole.

While the use of industry as a subject for a major fresco cycle in the heart of a major urban art museum can be considered in cultural and aesthetic terms to be a modern revolutionary act, it was not a call to political action. Rivera did not expect the murals to incite workers to take up arms against their capitalist employers. Nor did he expect the workers to acquire the means of production. The equal representation of worker and industrialist on the west wall suggests the interdependence of the two. Rivera internalized the lessons taught by Vasconcélos in the 1920s to use the arts to ameliorate social change. What he did expect in Detroit, as he had learned in Mexico, was that the tools of cultural nationalism could lead to greater acceptance between the classes, which created hope for a socialist state.

Finding the Detroit murals lacking in Marxist conviction, some viewers have tried to understand them through the lens of Freudian psychology. The intertpretation of the north and south wall automotive panels as a vagina and womb is based on a masculine misreading of the industrial processes.[7] The actual direction of the conveyors in the center of the north wall composition is toward the viewer, not away from the viewer. The interpretation of the engine blocks as semen moving away from the viewer to the blast furnace in the background is reversed. And, if the action is reversed, then the "vagina" is giving birth to the engine blocks, which biologically could not represent semen but would have to represent an egg or a fetus. Thus, the north wall "vagina" is giving birth into the direction of the viewer. The identification of the south wall as the womb is based on the female nature of the stamping press/Coatlicue. In reality Coatlicue is androgynous and performs both a life-giving and life-destroying function in the Aztec cosmos. The single-sex symbolism of the south wall as womb limits the larger vision that encompasses the duality not only of gender but of class, economics, culture, and nature vs. technology. Once again, a single interpretation according to sexual analogy, like the solitary Marxian reading, does not encompass the universal vision of Rivera.

An important distinction also needs to be made between Rivera's murals and the official state art, social realism, that emerged in the Soviet Union. "Vasconcélos' theory that art had to inform, interest, and inspire the people to serve the revolution" did not include propagandizing for the state. While Mexican muralism—especially that of Rivera—"was born as a pro-revolutionary art, it did not simultaneously emerge as the official state art."[8] Especially in the Detroit murals, Rivera made his own selection of subjects and style. Rivera believed that Henry Ford set the scene for a new socialist society through the creation of collective work on the assembly line. But Rivera placed that utopian society within the ancient context of the ritual of human sacrifice. The new society is at once the culmination of technological developments and an ancient ritual that is dominated by a cyclical sense of time, determinism, and cosmic power and order. Modern industry rests within the archetypal context of an ancient cosmology. Whether Rivera consciously tried to avoid a clear political ideology in Detroit is unclear. However, the end result is that he synthesized seemingly contradictory beliefs to present an image of hope. "In making his work utopian, Rivera, in his own mind, saved his ideological contradictions for he could through them exalt many of the political principles which he had always defended without committing himself to concrete facts which could have put his artistic career in danger."[9]

It is significant to compare Rivera's self-portrait in the *Detroit Industry* cycle to his earlier fresco self-portraits at the Secretaría and in San Francisco. Until Detroit he depicted himself as a worker. In Detroit he portrayed himself as an observer (see fig. 238) and, as such, placed himself in a class apart from the workers. In 1920, he had signed a manifesto declaring the superiority of public

238. Self-portrait of the artist, detail of the north wall automotive panel, fresco. Rivera included an inconspicuous portrait of himself wearing a bowler hat in the upper left corner. This is the first fresco portrait where he represented himself as an observer instead of a worker.

mural painting over easel painting, demanded the pay of a plasterer, and donned overalls. His public persona was that of a worker aligned to the working class. Thirteen years later in Detroit his role changed from worker to ambassador. He so believed in the efficacy of public art in general and his own fresco imagery in particular that he painted messages of amelioration and hope in *Detroit Industry*. He saw himself as a link between the Latin American south and the industrialized north bringing a vision of the continuity of culture in the Americas through native traditions. His depiction of a pre-Depression image of the Rouge—the Rouge of the golden industrial era—suggests that he also saw himself as a link between the industrialists and the workers. The fact that the images of the interior of the Rouge factories were painted in the heart of Detroit's temple of culture, which was built upon the backs of laborers depicted in the fresco, was both a reproach from the former revolutionary artist who, before he arrived in Detroit, called himself a guerrilla, and a gesture of reconciliation. Just as *tlacuilos* were requested by Catholic missionaries to make careful illustrations of banned human sacrifices as part of a means of legitimizing their presence in Mexico, so Rivera brought dreaded industry and the laborer into the high culture of the museum to introduce and legitimize cultural reality for the working class.

Rivera's seemingly disparate ideologies of communism, socialism, industrial determinism, ancient ritual sacrifice, and a fictive golden age of industry are well synthesized and orchestrated in *Detroit Industry*. He presented an ancient American context within which to understand the nature of modern industrial work by making an analogy between the Mexican archeological sites of human sacrifice and modern industry. Workers not only carry out an important ritual sacrifice of energy to sustain the order of the industrial cosmos, but they are themselves godlike. Rivera deified the multiracial work force through the images of the four races. He not only elevated the worker but he offered a way for all classes to understand and accept modern technology. He gave Detroit a new vision of itself by painting Henry Ford's concept of industrial determinism. The evolution of technology that he depicted as beginning in primordial agricultural production culminated in the modern assembly line. Rivera's *Detroit Industry* fresco cycle created a historical continuum that offered all classes a way to understand, appreciate, and legitimize modern industry, and to integrate it into their lives as an aesthetic, economic, technological, social, and political reality.

With this in mind, Rivera's own description of the murals makes greater sense than previously presumed when read from his utopian perspective.

> In the composition of the large wall on the right, the main currents of the composition come together in the center of the lower portion, in the midst of huge presses, in a realistic and abstract plastic, dynamic and everlasting, like the marvelous morphological representations of the Nahuatl cosmogony of earliest pre-historic America, that historic substratum into which plunge the roots of our continental culture, now on the eve of an artistic blossoming-forth through the union of the genius of the South, coming from the depths of the North, to produce the new human expression which shall be born in Greater America, where all races have come together to produce the new worker.[10]

VITA BREVIS LONGA ARS

"Rivera Was a Jolly Lad"

At last the job was finished and
The people flocked inside,
The clergy took one hasty look
And they were horrified!
They pointed shaking fingers at
The panel of diseases,
And said the vaccinated child
Was no one else but Jesus!
Oh, jolly old Diego,
His enemies abound-o
That most prodigious, sacrilegious,
Son-of-a-gun Diego!

These lyrics are taken from a song written in 1933 by Franklin M. Peck, assistant managing editor of the *American Boy/Youth's Companion Magazine*.[1] By the time they were written, the worst period of the *Detroit Industry* mural controversy was over. The song not only pokes fun at the artist, the murals, and their critics, but it also summarizes the salient issues of the controversy. Rivera was a Mexican who was commissioned to paint a "portrait" of Detroit when many artists in Michigan and the United States were out of work during the Depression. The artist was an avowed Communist who painted realistically. He painted the working classes instead of the Daughters of the American Revolution. The female nudes on the east wall were called pornographic. The *Vaccination* panel was labeled by the religious right as sacrilegious. And the artist was labeled "fistic" and charged with deliberately intending to provoke Detroiters with his images in the murals.

Rivera was just finishing the first ten panels of the upper registers of the murals when the first sensational newspaper article appeared on Sunday, October 23, 1932, in the *Detroit Times*:

From what is already on the walls, and from the sketches . . . the work in material, manner, and enormity is beyond the conception of the people outside the red drapes that cover the finished portions of the wall. [The drapes did not cover the frescoes, only the entrances to the court.] When they see it, it will hit them like a bolt.

In general, local and national publicity was positive throughout the time Rivera was in Detroit. Mexican revolutionary art was enthusiastically promoted in the United States by Mexicanophiles such as Anita Brenner (a writer who acted as Rivera's secretary) during the winter of 1932–1933.[2] Wayne State University's newspaper, the *Detroit Collegian*, ran an article almost every month reporting the progress of the artist's work at the Detroit Institute of Arts.[3]

Detroiters had other concerns in the winter of 1932–1933. In January, after Briggs Manufacturing, a medium-sized company supplying auto bodies to Ford and Chrysler, had sped up production by a third and cut wages by two-thirds, six thousand workers went on strike. Some fifteen thousand auto workers in plants throughout the Detroit area struck in sympathy, paralyzing automobile production for over two months until workers were forced to return to work in March. Walter Briggs, owner of Briggs Manufacturing, blamed the Communist Party for the strike. While the striking workers could not prevent the automobile corporations from hiring scab labor, the strike did help dramatize poor working conditions, and it was a turning point in creating widespread support for union organization. On February 14, 1933, Detroit's banking system collapsed when loans from bankrupt companies could not be collected. The bank closings in

239. Rivera (in lower left with white palette) completing the *Detroit Industry* murals, March 13, 1933.

Detroit created a chain reaction of bank failure across the nation. Franklin Delano Roosevelt was inaugurated as president in March and Congress quickly enacted many New Deal reforms to bring relief to the entire country.[4]

While the effects of the auto workers' strike and bank closings ripped through the already economically depressed city, Rivera continued to work steadily on the murals. During the month of January he took only one day off: New Year's Day. On February 19, 1933, the cartoons for the murals were publicly displayed at the museum. The day after, Valentiner received a resolution from the Detroit Catholic Students Conference requesting that committees be appointed by the Holy Name Society, the Knights of Columbus, and the League of Catholic Women to investigate the Rivera murals and, "if evidence warrants, to protest against their retention on the tax-paid walls of this institution."[5] While the director was surprised to receive this letter, he viewed it as an isolated incident, since no other negative public attention was given to the murals at that time. He had just returned to Detroit after his voluntary unpaid eight-month leave in Europe and was enraptured by the work that Rivera had carried out in the Garden Court while he was gone. Little did Valentiner know what was in store for him and the museum.

Rivera was anxious to start on his Rockefeller Center commission. Kahlo could hardly wait to leave Detroit and return to New York, where she could socialize with her friends and find all the necessary ingredients for Mexican cuisine. The major players in the mural project were all eagerly awaiting the completion date, which occurred on March 13, 1933 (fig. 239).

Suddenly, five days after Rivera finished the murals and four days before their public unveiling, attacks appeared in the press. On March 17, 1933, both the *Detroit News* and the *Detroit Evening Times* ran articles on the murals. The *Detroit News* quoted Reverend H. Ralph Higgins, senior curate of Saint Paul's Episcopal Cathedral, as saying that the "Vaccination Panel 'Held Caricature of Holy Family'; Officials Defend It." And in the *Evening Times* the headline read, "Rivera Mural Starts Fight." That day the museum received an anonymous telephone call from the American Citizens League complaining about the murals. The newspapers sensationalized this call and the headline in the March 18, 1933, *Evening Times* read, "Police Guard Rivera's Murals after Phoned Threat: Priest Calls One Subtle Blasphemy." The press had jumped in and the controversy began in earnest.[6]

An editorial in the March 18, 1933, *Detroit News* lambasted the murals, calling them "coarse in conception . . . foolishly vulgar . . . without meaning for the . . . intelligent observer . . . a slander to Detroit workingmen . . . un-American." The writer called for the murals to be whitewashed. All the social, political, and religious fears of the conservative Detroit community were summarized in the editorial. The Detroit establishment found themselves threatened by a major automobile workers' strike representing to them a rise in communism and reminding them of the economic and human deprivations of the Depression. Now a Mexican Communist artist had been paid to paint the working class in the factories on twenty-seven panels of a central three-story court of one of the most venerable institutions in the city.

March 21, 1933, was a busy day for Reverend Higgins of Saint Paul's. The morning *Detroit News* ran an article reporting that Valentiner had invited Higgins to the museum to look at the murals and discuss them. When they met, Valentiner apparently did not have much patience with him. In a letter to the director written later the same day, Higgins complained that Valentiner had spent very little time with him and that the museum director had misrepresented statements by the clergyman in that morning's news article.[7] The *Detroit Evening Times* of March 21, 1933, reported that Higgins had called a meeting of people opposed to the murals. In attendance were an architect, a structural engineer, three representatives of the art commission of the Detroit Review Club (the city's oldest women's club), two Catholic clergymen, one Episcopalian, and a lay member of the board of trustees of the Unitarian Church. It was described as "a volunteer group which has undertaken to crystallize feeling against the murals into a formal request that they be removed."[8]

March 21 was also a busy day at the Detroit Institute of Arts. The newly transformed Garden Court with its twenty-seven brilliantly painted panels was cleaned of plaster dust and opened to the public after having been closed for sixteen months. To many of the museum's regular visitors, it was a shock to see the grimy inside of the factories so dramatically represented in the middle of their elegant temple of art. To automobile workers, who had never seen themselves depicted in a cultural institution of the city, it was a revelation. And to the intellectual left, the murals held great hope for a new age.

On the evening of March 22, a group called the People's Museum Association held a public meeting on the murals in the Art Institute's Lecture Hall. The brainchild of Edsel Ford's assistant Fred Black and George Pierrot, a volunteer publicist for the Detroit Institute of Arts, the association, formed in September 1932, granted membership in the museum for a dollar a year instead of the ten dollars required by the Founders Society. Over three hundred people jammed the hall on the twenty-second, and individuals spoke out for several hours. The People's Museum Association continued to meet several more times in March and April. Petitions were signed. The media continued to fan the flames. "Socialites Elbow Laborers in Jam to View Murals," reported the *Detroit Evening Times* on March 22, 1933. "Battle Over Murals Draws Crowds to Institute of Arts," cried the same paper on March 23, 1933. "Hotter Waxes the Warfare Over the Murals of Diego," proclaimed an article in the *Detroit Free Press* of March 23, 1933, in which a meeting of the People's Museum Association, chaired by its president, Fred Black, was covered in detail.

Two days later, Councilman William P. Bradley presented a motion to the Detroit Common Council (the legal authority ultimately responsible for the municipal art museum) proposing that the "paintings be washed from the walls."[9] Before the Riveras had left for New York on March 14, 1933, the artist gave an interview saying that the murals were the finest work of his career and he hoped that they would not be destroyed. No action was taken on the motion.

Valentiner, E. P. Richardson, and those of the DIA staff who had survived layoffs of the previous year resulting from a severe reduction in the museum budget, ordered by the Detroit City Council, were frantically trying to counter the attack. Valentiner sent telegrams to directors of other art museums and members of the College Art Association asking for letters of support.[10] He gave a radio interview describing each panel of the murals in loving detail. He worked with George Pierrot on a booklet describing the murals. It was published the week of the opening. Besides giving a detailed description of each fresco panel based on the artist's own interpretation, Richardson and Pierrot added statements in the booklet that shed the most positive light on the subjects of the murals and on the artist. The style of the new murals was "monumental realism" (i.e., they are not Communist propaganda); the automotive panels "create so much space that the Garden Court seems larger and more restful than before the walls were painted" (i.e., they are not a visual cacophony of machines and workers); "from early March [*sic*] until the end of July [Rivera] visited automobile

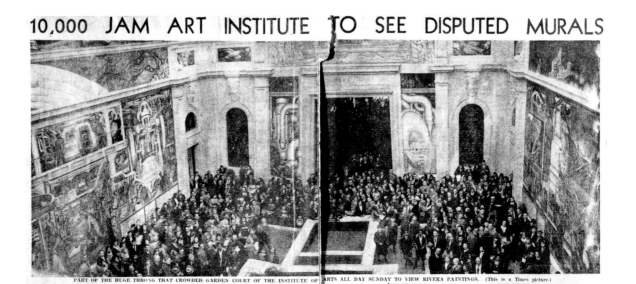

PART OF THE HUGE THRONG THAT CROWDED GARDEN COURT OF THE INSTITUTE OF ARTS ALL DAY SUNDAY TO VIEW RIVERA PAINTINGS. (This is a Times picture.)

240. "10,000 Jam Art Institute to See Disputed Murals," *The Detroit Times*, March 26, 1933.

factories and industrial plants . . . and went to the Michigan State Fair to draw animals." (i.e., how could an artist who was so dedicated to learning about Detroit and strove for such accuracy and who did not attend the hunger marches or picket lines of the strikes be a dangerous radical leftist?). Other defensive arguments were put forward: "Detroiters have admired Rivera's leadership in the movement to return impoverished Mexican laborers in the United States to their native soil. Rivera feels that these men, having learned a great deal in America, will make splendid citizens for Mexico. He feels that their departure will ease unemployment in this country." Arts Commissioner Albert Kahn gave a positive interview to the press the day after the opening. "There is nothing new in these attacks by churchmen. Michelangelo portrayed as devils the churchmen who tried to interfere with him when he was doing the Sistine Chapel. You can see their portraits today in the Sistine frescoes. Rembrandt was just as guilty of charges of sacrilege as Rivera. But who throws stones at Rembrandt today?"[11]

Throughout the week, the attacks and counterattacks escalated and so did attendance at the museum. An editorial in the March 23, 1933, *Detroit Free Press* proclaimed, "It is easy to understand the concern and disgust of members of Christian bodies over the grotesquerie and even blasphemy in the Diego Rivera murals. . . . Certainly they represent decadent art. Undoubtedly they contain communist propaganda. . . . The murals certainly cannot be taken seriously. But they might be kept as a historical curiosity—an example of the shallow thinking which was prevalent in this country."

Other organizations were quickly formed to support the murals. The Reverend Augustus P. Reccord, minister of the First Unitarian Church, spoke in favor of the murals against the advice of his own trustees. Labor and radical organizations and college students circulated and signed petitions, which are preserved in the museum archives. There was a swell of interest and enthusiasm for the murals that countered the hostile press and the Detroit Common Council's recommendations to whitewash them.

As the week progressed, attendance at the museum continued to soar. On Sunday, March 26, 1933, ten thousand people arrived to view the murals (fig. 240). That afternoon E. P. Richardson was recruited (as the only professional staff member whose native language was English) to speak to the crowd. He climbed up into an empty pool of the fountain so that he could be seen and lectured to the visitors about the murals. Richardson was touched to see a small group of staff members waiting anxiously below him to retrieve him if the crowd turned angry. He was pleasantly surprised to find a captive audience. The visitors politely listened and looked and the mild-mannered Richardson escaped unscathed.[12]

The controversy continued through April on a national level. Rivera was quoted in *Art Digest*: "The official Communist party of this country has expelled me from membership; and now the conservative element attacks me. However, my public is made up of the workers—the manual and intellectual workers. The religious are attacking me because I am religious; I paint what I see. Some society ladies have told me they found the murals cold and hard. I answer that their subject is steel, and steel is both cold and hard."[13]

In the same issue of *Art Digest*, the National Women's Division of the American Artists Professional League published an open letter: "had [the City of Detroit Arts Commission] heeded the requests of the women and had engaged one of our own mural painters to do the work," there would be no controversy; "now that the deed is done, however, every effort must be made to prevent the murals' destruction."[14]

On March 24, 1933, Valentiner had issued a defense of the murals stating that "Edsel Ford, the donor was, completely satisfied. . . . I am thoroughly convinced the day will come when Detroit will be proud to have this work in its midst. In the years to come they will be ranked among the truly great art treasures of America."[15] Valentiner sought a special meeting of the Arts Commission to draft a report to the Common Council saying that Rivera's murals were under attack because of work he had done elsewhere, not "because of what is here; that these were great works of twentieth-century art: and the City should keep them and be proud of them."[16]

On April 11, 1933, another meeting of the Arts Commission was convened. After hearing Valentiner's presentation, the commissioners voted unanimously to accept the murals. Edsel Ford was quoted the next day as saying, "I admire Rivera's spirit. I really believe he was trying to express his idea of the spirit of Detroit."[17] Rivera's biographer Bertram Wolfe observed that "feeble as these words were, they were a great help in saving the paintings."[18] Ford's words helped to stop the media attacks and quell the controversy. When Father Coughlin, the priest of the Shrine of the Little Flower Catholic Church, began to condemn the murals on his radio programs, other conservative religious leaders fell silent, not wanting to be associated with the extreme radical right. By the beginning of May, hostile letters to the editors only occasionally appeared in the Detroit papers, and the national press consistently stood behind the museum.

Valentiner later recalled, "I was never able to find out exactly how the attacks started. They came from Protestant as well as Roman Catholic sources, and they were connected with rumors to the effect that Rivera's paintings in a public building were blasphemous. The curious fact was that these rumors were circulated long before the murals were shown to the public."[19]

Valentiner could have questioned Edsel Ford, George Pierrot, and Fred Black. In January, Ford had asked Black to help publicize the museum in the wake of its budget cut. Where the museum had operated with $400,000 in, for example, 1928, it was allocated only $40,000 in 1933. Ford was personally providing funds to support the director, curators, and the mural project. He feared that the museum was about to lose even more support from the city. Ford wanted Black "to awaken some public interest in" the museum "and convince the City Council that they should do something about it. They feel that very few people go there, and the general public's not interested."[20] Black complied by putting the People's Museum Association to work. He and Pierrot had succeeded in attracting the working class with the new membership policy. Then, according to Black, "just out of the sky came a grand opportunity to get the Museum on the front page."[21] Someone had mentioned to Pierrot that an Episcopal clergyman thought that the *Vaccination* panel was a travesty of the Christian Holy Family. Pierrot organized an informal press conference on March 16, 1933, and invited members of the clergy to express their reactions to the murals. "It broke in the Detroit papers, and within ten days, was all over the world."[22]

Black explained that at meetings "anybody could talk for two minutes about the Rivera murals. They had to stay on the subject of the murals. We held a stopwatch, and they had to stop at the end of two minutes whether they were through or not. We soon had that hall overflowing at every meeting. There was always enough said at every meeting that newspaper men there would spot certain people and get little interviews. We kept that pot boiling for three or four weeks."[23]

The People's Museum Association grew rapidly to almost five thousand members. Clyde Burroughs, secretary to the Arts Commission, took the lists of members' names to the Common Council to convince them of broad interest in the museum. Black kept Ford advised of all the meetings and publicity. "I would show him all these things, and in most cases, he'd laugh. He thought it was a great scheme. We'd accomplished the thing he'd wanted done."[24]

Was the mural controversy simply a hoax initiated by Edsel Ford and developed by Fred Black and George Pierrot? Was it a means to reduce Edsel's financial obligation to pay museum staff salaries? Would it have occurred regardless of Black's and Pierrot's efforts? Was Rivera deliberately baiting the clergy with the use of a nativity scene transformed by science? What impact did the controversy have on the public's and museum's attitude toward the murals?

The fact that the People's Museum Association was organized in September 1932 confirms Black's statement that it was organized while the murals were being painted.[25] As recorded by the association's secretary, M. J. Haass, "The People's Museum Association bears the same relationship to the Detroit Institute of Arts that an advertising department bears to a business. Its job is to 'sell' the Institute of Arts to the people of Detroit, to promote in every way possible the activities of the Institute."[26]

It is hard to believe that Valentiner didn't know how the controversy started. How could he not see a link between the People's Museum Association and the controversy? His misrepresentation to the press about his meeting with the Reverend Ralph Higgins demonstrates either his impatience with criticism of the murals or his complicity in the controversy.

Valentiner was in Europe on his unpaid leave when the People's Museum Association was organized. Richardson kept Valentiner informed about the activities of the museum by letter. If Richardson did not inform him of the People's Museum Association or he did not know about the rabble-rousing by Pierrot and Black, then Valentiner could have missed the connection. There is no indication that Richardson knew of George Pierrot's initial press conference to incite the clergy. Richardson also expressed puzzlement in 1978 about how the controversy started. He talked about the fact that the controversy was such a trial that once it was over he "closed the files on the murals and did not open them until [the author] called for an interview" nearly fifty years later.[27] It wasn't until 1986, when George Pierrot called the author and described how he began the controversy by inviting the clergy to express their criticism of the murals, that the events of the period became clear. According to Pierrot, Valentiner was never informed of these behind-the-scenes activities.

Although Edsel Ford was president of the Arts Commission when the mural commission was accepted, funded the project, opened the Rouge to the artist, and provided him with guides, visited Rivera often during the painting of the murals, and socialized with Rivera and Kahlo, he distanced himself from the mural project during the controversy and remained publicly silent. His silence is explained by Black's statement that Ford requested Black to bring public attention to the museum. As an initiator of museum publicity, Ford was not going to block a valuable avenue of attention. Ford further distanced himself from the mural project, according to Black, in regarding himself as simply the financial support of the project with no connection to the selection of the artist or the subject matter. One can imagine that Edsel Ford, who was an extremely good friend of William Valentiner, would also distance himself from the director during the controversy to avoid impeding the defense of the murals and revealing his own central role in their creation.

In the end, the controversy brought much attention to the museum and the murals. The Common Council's resolution to whitewash the murals never even came up for a vote.[28] Through the People's Museum Association, the museum had increased its popular support and gained a new source of membership. On April 18, 1933, the Common Council passed a $132,326 budget for the 1933–1934 fiscal year, up from the $40,000 budget of 1933, but still far below the $400,000 pre-crash budget. Edsel Ford no longer needed to underwrite the salaries of curators. In mid-May Clyde Burroughs wrote to Clifford Wight: "We easily won our battle over the Detroit frescoes and were really surprised to find that most of the letter-writing public and others taking an active part in the controversy were on our side."[29]

Rivera's politics and his publicity seeking are detestable.
But let's get the record straight on what he did here.
He came from Mexico to Detroit, thought our mass production industries and our technology
wonderful and very exciting, painted them as one of the great achievements of the twentieth century.
This came just after the debunking twenties when our own artists and writers had found nothing worthwhile
in America, and worst of all in America was the Middle West.
Rivera came and painted the significance of Detroit as a world city.
If we are proud of this city's achievements, we should be proud of these paintings
and not lose our heads over what Rivera is doing in Mexico today.

241. Museum director Edgar P. Richardson viewing the installation of a sign supporting the artist, 1952. Rivera created another controversy in 1952 when he painted a mural commissioned by the Mexican government that positively presented Stalin and the North Koreans as peacemakers. To avert a reaction to the artist in Detroit, Richardson posted a sign condemning Rivera's politics while supporting the *Detroit Industry* murals.

For many years, Rivera's mural cycle was an aesthetic orphan in the family of art works at the Detroit Institute of Arts. It took fifty years for the murals to become the subject of scholarly study; it was fifty years before the cartoons were discovered in storage and officially accessioned; and it was over sixty years before the murals were cleaned and repaired. They were overlooked by several generations of modern art curators at the museum and by other scholars of modern art both in the United States and Mexico. With no public interpretation of the murals by the museum or the scholarly community there was no aesthetic context in which to place them. Consequently, the murals belonged to anyone who claimed them, including the Communist Party, who, as mentioned earlier, used the murals to win new members; civil rights leaders, who sought support from the working class; and corporate executive recruiters. Most of all, the murals were claimed by the public, whose interest made them the most popular work in the collection.

Lacunae in scholarship and interpretation of the murals are due to several factors, including the 1933 controversy, Rivera's political exploits after he left Detroit, and the reluctance of art historians who saw the Detroit mural cycle as ugly and/or politically inspired. Many factors contributed to the marginalization of the murals in modern art literature. The 1933 controversy increased museum attendance but also indelibly politicized the murals and the museum. The murals, and subsequently the museum, came to represent major social, economic, political, technological, and religious conflicts in the city. Most urban art museums are not the fulcrum of societal conflict, even though works of art are known for reflecting contemporary life. Rarely is a city's art museum so in tune with urban strife. In 1933 this major work of art was commissioned by the museum from an artist who not only understood the cultural fabric of the city but succeeded in painting a permanent vision of it on the four walls of the museum's central court. The controversy made the entire city—not just visitors to the museum—aware of its political issues. From that moment on the murals became politicized and rarely seen as works of art.

Rivera continued to become embroiled in controversies throughout his career. In his 1933 work at Rockefeller Center, *Man at the Crossroads Looking with Hope and High Vision to the Choosing of a New and Better Future,* he included a portrait of Lenin. The rental agents could not tolerate a portrait of a Communist leader in the lobby of their landmark new office building, whose space would be hard to rent during the height of the Depression. Abby Aldrich Rockefeller and her son Nelson, who had originally supported Rivera for the New York mural, did not argue with the agents. Nelson Rockefeller asked Rivera to remove the portrait of Lenin, but the artist refused. Rivera was trying for acceptance once again by the Communist Party and believed that his stance would put him in the party's good graces. Meanwhile, he alienated his patrons. The mural was covered, and several weeks later it was destroyed by the rental agents.[1]

The battle of Rockefeller Center did not lead to Rivera's readmission to the Communist Party, but nineteen years later another mural and controversy did gain him membership. In 1952 he was commissioned to paint a mural for a Mexican art exhibition in Paris organized by the Instituto Nacional de Bellas Artes in Mexico City. The mural, *The Nightmare of War and the Dream of Peace,* presented Stalin and Mao Tse-tung as purveyors of peace and South Koreans hanging, shooting, and whipping Communist North Koreans.[2] Rivera was featured in the international press for his support of two Communist leaders who were the most dreaded by fiercely democratic and nationalistic Americans in the post–World War II United States. This was at the beginning of the Cold War, when Stalin set up Soviet governments in Bulgaria, Czechoslovakia, East Germany, Hungary, Poland, and Romania. It was at the height of the Korean War, when Stalin supported the North Koreans with Russian troops and the United States joined other Western countries to form the North Atlantic Treaty Organization, a mutual defense organization against Russia. It was also the beginning of the McCarthy hearings in the United States Senate, charging that Communists had infiltrated the government.

The atrocities of Stalin's anti-Semitic purges had surfaced in the international press. In reaction, the Communist Party was attempting to reverse the image of Stalin as executioner. Rivera's thirty-three-by-fifteen-foot mural on war and peace presented Stalin as the "apostle of peace and the hope of mankind. Stalin the Terrible had been overpainted with a portrait of Stalin the Good."[3]

Rivera had a long history with the Mexican Communist Party. Expelled in 1929 for disobedience to its policies, he had repeatedly and unsuccessfully petitioned for readmission. With this mural Rivera symbolically made another petition to rejoin the party.[4] After pleading unsuccessfully with the artist to remove the offending portrait, the organizers of the exhibition (Fernando Gamboa and the composer Carlos Chávez) officially rejected it. The Mexican Communist Party rallied to the cause. It set up a public viewing of the mural, which was "more a political demonstration than an art show. Leaders of the Communist Party, fellow-traveler intellectuals, Communist artists, officials of the Mexican Peace Committee [who had attended Stalin's Stockholm Peace Petition, meeting diplomats from iron curtain countries supporting Communist North Koreans who invaded South Korea in 1950], all rallied in support of the exhibition."[5]

By creating such a blatantly propagandistic mural, which he had executed in secret and then publicly defended after its rejection by the Bellas Artes, Rivera became a political embarrassment to Mexico and to all his patrons, including those associated with the Detroit Institute of Arts. E. P. Richardson, who by 1952 was director of the Detroit Institute of Arts, anticipated a controversial reaction in Detroit to the current events in Mexico. He had a large sign made supporting the aesthetic and historical importance of the *Detroit Industry* murals and displayed it at the east end of Rivera Court (fig. 241).[6] Councilman Eugene Van Antwerp threatened to whitewash the murals, and the City Council asked for a response from the Arts Commission.[7] To Richardson's surprise, he received only a few letters protesting the murals and realized he could have saved the cost of making the enormous sign in defense of *Detroit Industry*.[8]

Rivera's artless propaganda with the *Nightmare* painting in 1952 did not generate a large following in the United States, Mexico, or Europe. The Cold War was on and the mural looked like a missive from enemy territory. In addition, at that time realism was out of fashion in the American art world, and abstract expressionism was in vogue. It was the first major modern art movement to originate in the United States after World War II, when New York displaced Paris as the previously uncontested center of the visual arts in the west. Art historians such as Meyer Shapiro, who had championed Rivera's work in the early 1930s, had completely shifted perspective by the 1950s to support abstract expressionism. When this highly subjective, personal, nonrepresentational, expressionistic, and apolitical art came to be accepted, suddenly Rivera's 1930s murals began to appear ugly, naïve, and politically embarrassing. Their subject was not clearly political enough to inspire public action against them, nor was their 1930s realism championed strongly enough to create a *cause célèbre* in the art world.

From the 1950s through the 1970s, Rivera Court was used variously as a special exhibition gallery for modern sculpture, a smoking lounge, and a reception and dining hall. To the novice visitor, the murals dominated any sculptural objects placed in the court. But to the museum curators and patrons, the murals were often invisible. By the 1970s, the condition of Rivera Court was beginning to deteriorate. The skylight leaked and water had damaged the feet of the black race figure. The wooden beams of the ceiling were so brittle that electricians could no longer walk out on them to replace the floodlights: hence the murals were poorly lit. A fine layer of tar from tobacco smoke covered the frescoes with a gray shroud.

Another controversy over the *Detroit Industry* murals attracted media attention in 1979. This time Rivera's politics were unrelated to the issue. The director of the Detroit Institute of Arts, Frederick J. Cummings, envisioned Rivera Court as the hub of a new physical axis connecting the north and south wings of the museum through the center of the original 1927 building. With the additions of these two wings in the 1960s, the clarity and symmetry of circulation originally established in the old building was obscured. Cummings attempted to solve this problem. He hired the Detroit architectural firm of William Kessler and Associates to develop ideas. Part of the solution proposed was to open the floor of Rivera Court and install a stairwell in the center to connect the main floor of the museum to the lower level. The design called for a discreet chrome and glass railing surrounding glass stairs. When the plan was made public, preservationists in the Detroit community and on the museum staff objected to the stairwell on several grounds: its construction could damage the murals, and it certainly would be a permanent disruption to the contemplative atmosphere of Rivera Court, creating an obstacle to viewing the murals and reducing them to decoration.[9]

The stairwell proposal epitomized the museum's historical neglect of the murals. Preservationists interpreted the proposal as a potential act of vandalism. Cummings, an art historian whose specialty was European baroque and rococo painting, was a visionary who professionalized the DIA but he never publicly warmed to the aesthetic possibilities of Rivera's idiom or ideology. In seeking support for the stairwell project from other directors of art museums, his own sentiments were echoed by National Gallery of Art director J. Carter Brown's response to the murals: "Historically, the Rivera Court is already rather charmingly anomalous—modern and native American cultures in an Italianate Beaux-Arts Renaissance revival architectural setting is already a precedent."[10] In response to the outpouring of protest, the unfortunate stairwell proposal was set aside indefinitely by the Arts Commission.

Perhaps because the murals are a permanent part of the walls of the court, but more likely because they represent a style and era of art that quickly fell out of favor, no curatorial department within the museum took responsibility for them. They did not receive the professional care and attention normally given all other works in the collection, such as daily checks by security and curatorial staff for any changes in condition. Before the conservation laboratory was established at the Detroit Institute of Arts in the early 1970s, a series of painting restorers were called in to touch up the murals. They left traces of oil paint, although oil is a medium incompatible with fresco. No curatorial department pursued research and publication. As a work of art, the *Detroit Industry* murals were in museological limbo. Scores of sculpture and design exhibitions were installed in Rivera Court, as if there was nothing of importance on the walls. Formal dances, dinners, and receptions regularly took place in the space without any thought of protecting the frescoes.

Over the years, several physical changes have been made to Rivera Court.

242. Rivera's assistant Stephen Dimitroff cleaning his portrait in the fresco, 1988.

In 1957 the Detroit architectural firm of Suren Pilafian was hired to remove the large 1930 stone fountain and install a small fountain at the east end of the court. The original floor made of brick paving, slate, and black stone was removed and a terrazzo floor installed. As mentioned earlier, in 1987 and 1988 the murals were cleaned by Lucienne Bloch and Stephen Dimitroff under the supervision of the DIA's Conservation Services Laboratory. They sponged the surface of the murals with distilled water and removed the coating of dirt that had obscured the colors. Outside of the damage to the black race figure and minor paint losses, the frescoes were found to be in remarkably good condition. Later that year, with the encouragement of Samuel Sachs II, the director of the DIA, Barbara Heller, director of the Conservation Services Laboratory, secured funds for the renovation of the skylight and the replacement of the floor of the court with ceramic tile from Detroit's Pewabic Pottery that matched the design of the original floor of the adjacent Great Hall. With the replacement of the floor, the small fountain installed in 1957 was also removed.

In his later years William Valentiner "always considered 'The Mexican Adventure' the high point of his career."[11] His hopeful prediction that the murals would be seen as the greatest modern art work to address industry has only recently been realized by art historians such as Francis O'Connor and Gerald Silk and art critics such as Max Kozloff.[12] Following the fall of the Berlin Wall in 1989, a member of the intellectual left interpreted the murals as "politically wanting."[13]

Thus, the *Detroit Industry* murals have been ignored by the art critics during the Cold War as being too political and now by the left as politically wanting. Each era has made a reading of the murals based on the changing political climate, not based on the actual content of the murals. David Craven has proposed a reason why Rivera's work appealed to both capitalists and workers. Capitalists saw the depiction of modern industry in Rivera's murals as the continuation of present industrial production in the future, and workers saw the depiction of the present as a means to a different and better future. Opposite ends of the political spectrum were able to see their own reality in the murals because of Rivera's fidelity to an ideal present.[14]

In many respects Rivera's sojourn in the United States fits the assimilation model of immigrants. His expulsion from the Mexican Communist Party in 1929 dramatized the political conflict he had been in for some time. The conflict was actually between his public persona as a revolutionary artist and his livelihood on the government dole. His membership in the Communist Party affirmed his public persona but did not inform his political beliefs. He was in a self-imposed exile when he left Mexico to paint in the United States. By the time he reached Detroit two years later, after having completed three murals in San Francisco and a solo exhibition at the Museum of Modern Art, the United States had not only become a haven for work but also provided the high lifestyle he enjoyed. Rivera was so content in the United States that Frida feared that he would never want to leave. The clues to his assimilation are identical to his newly appropriated identity in the Detroit murals. He no longer needed to identify himself with the worker. He could now portray himself as the actual observer he was at the Ford Motor Company for a month before he began to paint. The Detroit fresco cycle, unlike the Mexican murals, are not a call to action. Nowhere in *Detroit Industry* do we find a vision of the new society made up of the soldier, the worker, and the farmer. Instead, Rivera emphasizes a cultural synthesis and a synergistic relationship between the North and South Americas, between management and labor, and between the cosmic and technological order. The emphasis on the symbiotic relationship betwen the north and south also indicates a move away from the Marxist interpretation of the exploitation of the Mexican workers by capitalists in the United States. Rivera attempted to broaden the concept of American cultural history beyond the national borders of the United States by showing the interdependence of north and south. In this sense he expresses the American optimism of immigrants to his newly adopted land while at the same time remaining tied philosophically to his homeland. When he successfully appealed for government support in transporting Mexicans and Mexican Americans back to Mexico as part of the national deportation during the Depression, he was equally praised by the Mexican community as well as by the Detroit establishment. He was the celebrity lending his name and influence to a worthy cause between two countries. *Detroit Industry* represents a major paradigm shift in identity from the worker/revolutionary to the observer/ mediator. In that respect it represents a tremendous period of growth and maturation in his art that was all too short-lived. Once Rivera left Detroit to paint at the Rockefeller Center in New York, he was immersed in a politically charged environment and felt compelled to demonstrate his allegiance to the Communist cause.

It will take more years of political change to allow the public and scholars to see the murals outside of the political climate and assess them as works of modern art. "As an insight into the conditions of the modern working class, as an analysis of mass product assembly, with its support systems, planning, and processing, as a public and political document of the possibilities of technology, the epic Detroit frescoes have no peer in Western art."[15]

The *Detroit Industry* fresco cycle is one of the essential expressions of Detroit's cultural life. But it also characterizes an entire era. As such, it can be seen as it was conceived, as a totally integrated work of art that reaches far beyond the particularities of Detroit and speaks on a universal plane. The cycle reflects not only the essence of the industrial culture of Detroit but also belief in technology and science that is still operative today. As such, it is a history-making work of art in which the working class and industrialists both find affirmation. Imagine the Detroit Institute of Arts without the Rivera fresco cycle at its center. No other work of art in the collection connects to the industrial, technological, and scientific realities of the city. And no other work of art of the twentieth century so clearly embodies the ideals, aesthetic preferences, and realities of industrial technology during that brief period of time between the Depression and the beginning of World War II.

As a didactic work of art, the *Detroit Industry* fresco cycle had many imitators in the Works Progress Administration mural project and in the black and Hispanic protest murals of the 1960s. Rivera's realistic style, utopian ideals, and the public nature of his art had a tremendous impact in the 1930s and the 1960s. While fresco as a medium has had revivals in New York, Chicago, and Los Angeles in the last fifty years, the concept of large-scale public art has been taken up by other artists, particularly abstract expressionists.

Rivera created a history for Detroit that is as rational and optimistic as the positivism of the Diaz era of his youth in Mexico. Detroit's own natural resources and its geographic location on a river are the basic reasons for its place in modern industry. Its multiracial work force represents the entire scope of humanity and all the positive characteristics of each race. Modern industry is an entity larger than the sum of its component parts; it is a system on a cosmic scale comparable to the Aztec notion of the universe. Ultimately, it is fueled by the sacrifice of human individuality and energy for the collective good.

Philosophically, Rivera provided Detroit with a context for its industrial reality. In this sense he performed a function that he, as a mature muralist, believed was his destiny. His role was part diplomat, as a Mexican artist in the United States. But he also performed as a cultural revolutionary. And this, beyond his politics as a Communist, was his real strength as an artist. By confronting Detroit with its industrial heritage in a deterministic historical perspective, he was both offering a context in which to understand a modern phenomenon and forcing a confrontation of the inherent social and economic dichotomies of the city. All these ideas are presented in the sophisticated visual language of his mature mural style. Gone are the idealistic worker larger than life in the California School of Fine Arts mural. In its place are realistic images of people at work but now choreographed in an industrial dance scored by the demands of the conveyor line. Gone are the simple grids in which to place images taken directly from Italian Renaissance murals. In its place are the writhing and undulating movements of the conveyors, which weave the industrial processes together while they push and pull the viewer's eyes forward and back into deep space.

In summarizing the importance of the *Detroit Industry* fresco cycle, Ida Rodriguez Prampolini's characterization of modern Mexican art is useful.

> 1) monumentality and miniturization; 2) the use of myth; 3) the necessity of dialogue, expression, and communication where the viewer participates to understand; 4) the importance of death and fate; 5) a proliferation of forms which multiply in a "disordered" fashion; 6) the importance of the artist's self-reflection; 7) the concept of the multiplicity of race; and 8) the appearance of what is considered tasteless because it is a hybrid and is exuberant . . .[16]

Prampolini's final characteristic item ("what is considered tasteless because it is a hybrid and exuberant") poses one of the great difficulties for traditional art historians, curators, and critics who criticize Rivera's mural style. Rivera turned away from abstraction, which has been considered an "anti-modern" act. He visually and stylistically quoted from disparate sources such as Italian Renaissance painting and pre-Hispanic Mexican sculpture. His mural style is seen by traditional art historians not only as *retardataire* but also as an unintegrated hybridization of styles and thus "ugly." Part of this conception is based on an unfamiliarity with the images, aims, and forms of modern art outside of Paris and New York. But it is also political. Art historians of Rivera's generation went through a radical change from a belief that art should express political and/or moral views to a total rejection of that concept when the formalist philosophy of Clement Greenberg and abstract expressionism came into vogue in the 1950s. Now it is clear that the realistic style Rivera used for his mature murals developed from the modern classical realist style, which many artists turned to in 1917 and 1918 in Paris after World War I. While Rivera and his fellow Mexican muralists publicly pronounced abstract easel painting to be inferior to the aesthetic and political relevance of modern realistic mural painting, they continued to incorporate their understanding and assimilation of modern European art forms into their revolutionary work.

It is also becoming clear that the Mexican muralists were not simple propaganda organs for their government and should not be categorized with the artists who did propagandize for Stalin, Hitler, and Mussolini. While the *Detroit Industry* murals served political purposes in marketing the museum to its public, assisting the Ford Motor Company's image in Detroit, and in paving the way for a new Ford factory in Mexico, Rivera worked entirely on another plane in creating the program for the fresco cycle.

Rivera reached a level of understanding about himself, his work, and the world that is reflected in the Detroit murals and that does not appear in any of his work before or after. This work was not to be equaled in the remainder of Rivera's career. In its Pan-American perspective, thematic richness, complexity of design, boldness of presentation, and vibrance of color, the Detroit mural cycle has no peer in the history of modern art. *Detroit Industry* remains today a historical record of a fictive past, a utopian vision of the industrial culture of Detroit played out on a cosmic scale, an inspiration to the entrepreneur and social reformer alike, and a monumental modern work of art to be contemplated, studied, and enjoyed.

NOTES

Preface

1. The Ford Archives, Henry Ford Museum, subsequently gave their set of negatives to the Detroit Institute of Arts.

2. Francis V. O'Connor, "The Diego Rivera Murals," unpublished lecture presented at the Detroit Institute of Arts on March 20, 1977. Photocopy.

3. Letter from Frida Kahlo to Clyde Burroughs, May 20, 1933, Burroughs files, Museum Archives, The Detroit Institute of Arts.

4. Dolores Olmedo turned her home and collection into the Museo Dolores Olmedo Patiño in 1996, with three pavilions devoted to works by Diego Rivera, Frida Kahlo, and Mexican popular art.

Introduction

1. See Cordero in Oles 1993 for a discussion of the politics and philosophy of the Vasconcélos era.

2. See Delpar 1992, 12.

3. Babson et al. 1986, 27.

4. See Sterne 1980, 178–222.

5. Ibid., 77.

6. Babson et al. 1986, 52.

7. See Downs 1978, 47–52.

8. For thoughtful insights, see Hurlburt 1989 and Catlin in Detroit 1986, which are both based on Detroit 1978; for Marxian fiction and sexual fantasy, see Smith 1993.

9. Ibid.

10. Delpar, 1992

11. Wood 1992, 2.

12. Detroit 1986; McMeckin 1986.

13. Brown in Detroit 1986

14. With the disintegration of the Soviet Union in the early 1990s, Marxist art historians now seem to be seeking failure in every art work with leftist political content that they previously had extolled for those very same qualities. The Detroit murals are criticized as lacking in socialist content and ineffective in prompting political action or in attracting ideologically similar artistic followers, as well as being declared decidedly unmodern in style. See Smith 1993, 199–246.

15. Charlot 1979, 316.

Chapter One

1. Helen Wills recalled: "In Detroit after the game was over, my mother and I went to see the Art Institute, which is well known for its paintings and their unusually good arrangement. But we were too late. The doors had just been locked. We looked in and saw, dimly, some one moving about, who evidently saw us too, and came to open the door. It was the head of the institute, [William] Valentiner. It was a happy incident for me, since it was the start of a friendship which was to last many years.

"He is considered the world's first authority on Rembrandt, and is a student of art of every period. Since then, I have been to museums and galleries in New York, London, Berlin and Amsterdam with him, and have, in a way, viewed great paintings through the eyes of some one who knows everything about them. Even I, with my limited knowledge, could catch a glimpse of the final meaning or awareness as to what can be done by masters in paint and canvas. And it was made possible simply because we were late after the tennis and were looking through a locked door." Wills 1937, 123–124.

2. See Wilhelm [William] Reinhold Valentiner Papers, Microfilm Reel D31, 1931 Diary, 49. Archives of American Art, Washington, D.C.

3. "Rivera was allowed to climb on the high umpire-seat, where all alone he looked like an enormous Buddha. He was wiping his fore-head constantly, as the sun was strong and his head was turning back and forth following the ball game. He had a strong accent talking English and was happy to be able to talk French with me and we soon became friends." Wills 1937, 41.

4. Rivera 1934, 4.

5. Sterne 1973, 96–98.

6. Ibid.

7. Wight, n.d., box 1, February 5, 1931.

8. Richardson 1931, 76.

9. Valentiner files, DIA Museum Archives.

10. Letter from Diego Rivera to William Valentiner, May 2, 1931, DIA Museum Archives.

11. Paine 1931.

12. Certificate of Incorporation of Mexican Arts Association, Inc., Rockefeller Family Archives, RG (OMR), Cultural Interests Series, Box 107, Folder 961.

13. Letter from Kahlo to Clifford Wight and Jean Abbott Wight from New York, April 12, 1932; Mary Anne Martin Fine Art Gallery, New York.

14. Ibid.

15. Ibid.

16. Valentiner files, DIA Museum Archives.

17. "Many Detroiters, whatever their feelings about Communist leadership, must have taken grim satisfaction in the choice of target. For by 1932, Henry Ford had lost much of the prestige and public support initially generated by his Model T car and the $5-a-day profit sharing. . . . he stubbornly refused to update the Model T or join the trend toward annual styling changes. . . . By 1927, when he finally shut down his plants to retool for a new line of cars, Ford had lost his dominant position in the industry. As competition intensified, Ford could not afford to pay workers twice as much as rival companies . . . [and produced] increasingly repressive labor policies. Where one foreman had previously supervised 30 workers, by mid-decade there was one per 15 workers. A penitentiary-like atmosphere dominated the company's plants: workers were prohibited from talking, whistling, or even humming on the job. Sitting was also prohibited. Some may have expected confrontation. The 69-year-old [Henry] Ford, in his increasing isolation and paranoid state of mind, publicly claimed that a Jewish conspiracy [of bankers and radicals] was responsible for his troubles. . . . After confronting and then passing a small contingent of Dearborn police at the city line, the protesters pressed up Miller Road. . . . As fireman prepared to douse the crowd with frigid water, the police threw tear gas. The crowd responded with rocks and pieces of coal from a nearby dump. Then suddenly, all hell broke loose. 'Through [Gate Three's] openings,' recalled Ray Pillsbury, a photographer for the *Detroit Mirror*, 'policemen and guards leveled their guns and pulled the triggers. I would guess that hundreds of shots were fired into the mob. I saw their leaders drop, writhing with their wounds, and the mob dropped back, leaving their casualties on the road.' " Babson 1986, 58–59.

18. Ibid., 60.

19. As quoted in Freedland 1987, 16.

20. Cruben 1932.

21. Sterne 1980, 194.

22. Halberstadt 1978.

23. Lepine Memoirs, Ford Archives. Michigan Governor William Comstock declared a bank holiday Tuesday, February 14, 1932. Edsel Ford's initial $10,000 for the two-panel project was lost in the bank closing. Thus Ford actually contributed $30,889 to the mural project.

24. *Figures relating to the decoration in fresco in the Detroit Institute of Arts.*

Two Main Panels, AA, 175.721 square yards

Narrow panels above them, FF, 42.961 square yards

Top panels above them, DD, 66.338 square yards

Two upright doorway panels, BB, 25.151 square yards

Panel over doorway and at balcony, EE, 25.379 square yards

Top panel over doorway, H, 25.499 square yards

Eight square panels, D, 54.127 square yards

Eight tile panels, G 12.187 square yards

Original Estimate, San Francisco:

Two main panels AA to section of gold,

108.6 square yards @ $100 a square yard $10.860.

Price agreed upon $10.000.

Two main panels AA painted to the bottom, 175.721 square yards for $10,000 is at 56.91 per sq. yard.

Figuring at this reduced price per square yard:

(A) Mr. Rivera has agreed to paint the two doorway panels, BB, free.

(B) I agree to carve the stone panels, KK, in relief from Mr. Rivera's designs, free.

(C) Mr. Rivera is not sure at present whether he will want to decorate the panels FF and the eight panels G, but if he does so, he will paint them free.

This leaves panels AA, CC, H, EE, and 8 D with a total area of 367.056 sq. yards.

367.056 sq. Yards @ $56.91 a square yard $20.889.

The total wall space covered by the murals is 447.855 square yards for an average amount of $27.52 per square yard.

Clifford Wight typewritten document in Box 1, Technical Documents, Clifford Wight Collection, University of Syracuse Library.

Chapter Two

1. Preliminary Work on Walls Prior to Rivera's Arrival

It will be necessary to furr out the present walls where frescoes are to be painted in the following manner:

Using standard U-section metal bars, the following dimensions ¹/₂ x 1" lengths of upright bars to extend from bottom to top, crossbars may be spliced forming a grid-work, both horizontally and vertically, with bars on 2' centers. These bars are to be attached to present brick wall with expansion bolts. It is essential that expansion bolt-holes be drilled through present plaster and well into the structural wall. Horizontal bars may be wired to vertical bars. Would suggest the use of diagonals to prevent possibility of sagging. This structural metal should be galvinized or sherardized. Galvinizing or sheradizing should be done in such a manner that work is free from pinholes, blisters or blowholes. Failure to do this successfully will result in rust eventually striking through the plaster and discoloring the fresco. Hence, this should be inspected carefully.

Metal lath, galvanized or sheradized to the same specification, is to be stretched over the furring and wired. All wiring must be galvanized or sheradized. As furring is

erected, it will be possible to correct any deviations from a plane surface. This should be inspected by the architect's office. Two coats of plaster are to be applied to these surfaces—the scratch coat to consist of 1¹/₂ parts of coarse white marble dust; 1 part electrically roasted and thoroughly slaked lime; 1 part Portland cement with sufficient (long) fibre to bind. After this coat has been applied the surface should be scratched. the second or brown coat should consist of two parts medium white marble dust; one part electrically-roasted, thoroughly slaked lime and short fibre. As this coat dries, it should be floated with a cork float. This coat should be floated level to a plane surface. [The] final coat [two coats] is applied from day to day, according to the necessities of the work. There should be available for the final coat, lime of the above description and fine white marble dust.

Scaffolding, Etc.

It will be necessary to remove all plants, flowerpots, sculpture, etc. from the side wall of the Indoor Court and it would be advisable to lower the present earth level to at least 6". Over the earth troughs lay 2 x 12 planks, building up the inside coping of the trough level with the outside, and fasten cleats as guides for the scaffolding rollers, in manner indicated on the accompanying sketches. Remove from court all plants and objects of art which may be affected by exposure to, or accidental dropping of lime.

A movable scaffolding should be built to conform to the accompanying sketches which are self-explanatory. Scaffolding should be constructed of finished lumber— free from pitch, knots, etc. There should also be provided at least 3 16 foot planks, 2¹/₂ x 14" for movable stages on the scaffolding. The rollers should be able to take care of 1000 pounds useful load.

Miscellaneous.

A white marble slab, preferably at least 2 x 4' [,] should be provided for the color grinder. It will be necessary to provide a work room with large drafting tables and benches for full-sized cartoons. This should be located as nearly as possible to the court. A supply of distilled water should be available for color-grinding and painting.

Albert Kahn, an architect and a member of the Art Commission at the time, was enlisted by Valentiner to gather some of the materials. Kahn had been the person responsible for bringing the Philadelphia architect Paul Cret to Detroit to design the new Detroit museum just a few years earlier. He was ambivalent, at best, about the massive changes to the still new Garden Court (interview with the architect's daughter, Lydia Winston Malbin, 1977), which was intended as a respite from art, a visual clearing of the palate. The prospect of large permanent murals completely reversed Cret's original intent.

Kahn was invaluable in seeing the project to a successful completion. He socialized with Rivera, Kahlo, and the Wights (letter from Kahn to Rivera inviting them to dinner, July 27, 1932, Wight Files, Box 1, Archives of the University of Syracuse Library). In the end, he invited Rivera to paint a mural for the General Motors Building at the 1933 Chicago World's Fair.

Kahn wrote to Clifford Wight on January 5, 1931, recommending the United States Gypsum Company as a source for the lime (letter from Albert Kahn to Clifford Wight January 5, 1932, Clifford Wight Collection, Syracuse University Library, Box 1. Valentiner files, DIA Museum Archives, and in the Wight n.d. box.

2. Ernst Halberstadt interview by the author, January 1978, Pocosset, Mass.

3. Ibid.

4. Ernst Halberstadt telephone interview by the author, January 1981.

5. Stephen Pope Dimitroff, panel discussion, the Detroit Institute of Arts, transcript, 1978, p. 26.

6. Valentiner files, DIA Museum Archives.

7. The only known Detroit artists who assisted with the murals were Winifred Grindley, Frank Stone, and Bob Rugovina. Grindley learned the fresco technique from Rivera. She is reported to have painted a portable fresco for the Thirtieth Annual Exhibition of the Detroit Society of Women Painters and Sculptors, held at the Scarab Club (an artist's club behind the Detroit Institute of Arts). Her fresco was not described but she was reported as "a pretty blond girl who has been assisting Diego Rivera" ("Artist Exhibit Opens Tonight," *Detroit Times,* January 28, 1933). Frank Stone originally studied art in his native city of New York. During the Depression he worked as an itinerant painter decorating businesses and bars with scenic murals of mountains and seascapes. Rivera hired him to enlarge drawings for the murals, and he worked for him throughout the mural project. Halberstadt remembered Bob Rugovina as mostly watching Rivera paint (Ernst Halberstadt interview by the author, January 1978). Another artist who watched Rivera intently while he painted was Sonya Cohen, who sculpted a portrait bust of the artist; *The Detroit News,* January 24, 1932.

8. Wolfe 1963, 288.

9. Sterne 1973, 96. Of Cristina Hastings, Lucienne Bloch recalled that she "was a fantastic Italian woman who always pushed [her husband] to become a great artist. She would bring back stacks of books from the library across the street, hoping he would read them and really get into this thing. And she and I had a

wonderful time. We went to baseball games and we went all over the place, ate hot dogs, we really slummed it" (Detroit 1978a).

10. See letters between Edsel Ford and Hastings; letter from Edsel Ford to United States Secretary of Labor W. N. Doak requesting extension of Hastings's visas, Edsel Ford Papers file #6, Ford Archives, Henry Ford Museum, box 386.

11. *The New York Times* April 2, 1933.

12. Ibid.

13. *Detroit Free Press*, January 7, 1933.

14. Ernst Halberstadt telephone interview by the author, March 1983.

15. Herrera 1983, 130.

16. "Rivera believed that women were just as good as men. And this was before women's lib. And he wasn't abashed to tell me, 'Lucy, you go there and enlarge the sketch for the woman, the big woman lying there on top, from a small sketch—an inch, to three feet.' He said, 'Glue the paper together, make it big enough so that it will fit in the space for them, and enlarge it.' And there I was. He never questioned that I couldn't do it. I was of course flattered and he gave me that much more courage" Bloch, in Detroit 1978a.

17. Dimitroff in Detroit 1983.

18. Ibid.

19. Ernst Halberstadt interview by the author, January 1978, Pocasset, Mass.

20. Ibid.

21. "I read an announcement that three artists had been chosen to decorate Radio City Lobby at Rockefeller Center— Sert, Brangwin and Rivera. I was familiar with one or two published books showing works of Rivera and I was greatly impressed by these. I had some drawings back in Massachusetts that were enormous cartoons on wrapping paper. I hitchhiked back to Boston (of course this was the Depression and I didn't have the money for railroad fare or bus fare); I rolled these enormous sheets of brown paper on a piece of wood and went back to New York without a nickel in my pocket. My father came running after me saying, 'You can't go without money . . . ' He thrust $5.00 into my hand and said, 'Here, you can live on that.' Well, that kept me going for two weeks in New York . . . " Halberstadt in Detroit 1978a.

22. Ibid.

23. Valentiner files, 1933.

24. Halberstadt interview, 1978.

25. Halberstadt remembered that Davis painted the predella panel. Stephen Dimitroff has refuted this story saying the Rivera painted all twenty-seven panels alone. Dimitroff was in New York when the panels were painted, preparing for the Rockefeller Center mural.

26. Fred L. Black, Oral History, Box 115, Ford Archives, Henry Ford Museum.

27. Wolfe 1963, 305; and Wight n.d., diary, box 1.

28. A typewritten work schedule is preserved among Clifford Wight's papers dating from the late fall or early winter of 1932 after Rivera received the Rockefeller Center mural commission (Wight n.d., box 1). The preliminary drawings and cartoons for New York were created during the time he was working on the Detroit murals. Thus Rivera was working on two mural projects at the same time.

The work schedule reads:

Sanchez 5 A.M. till 1 P.M.

Grinding color.

Sweep upstairs studios.

Miscellaneous.

Niendorf . . . 12 noon till 8 P.M.

Mix plaster.

Miscellaneous.

Halberstadt . . . After Museum closes at night.

Preparing full-size cartoon for Rockefeller Center Mural and ruling the squares etc. This work to be done on the floor of the main hall and rolled up and stored in the entrance to Garden Court during the day.

Wight 8 P.M. till 5 A.M. or when plaster is finished.

Work each day enlarging Rockefeller Center composition on full size cartoon till finished. After that, work each day on stone-cutting. [On the assumption that Diego is working between the hours of 5 A.M. and 8 P.M.]

Notes written in pencil at the bottom of the page:

Cheque from N.Y.?

Modification of shape of R.C. mural?

Edsel's portraits

Part of Wight's own plastering schedule is also preserved in his papers (box 1):

First Panel

Wednesday 25 11:15 A.M.–9:45 P.M. 10 1/2

Thursday 26 11 A.M.–5:30 P.M. TOO PATCHY

Friday 27 10:45 A.M.–9:45 P.M. 11

Saturday 28 11:30 A.M.–10:30 P.M. 11

Second Panel

Monday 30 11:30 A.M.–6:30 P.M. TOO DRY

Tuesday 1 12:30 A.M.–4 & 5:30–9:30 7 1/2

Wednesday 2 11 A.M.–5 P.M. & 6 P.M. to 6 A.M. PART LOST 18

Thursday 3 12 A.M.–6:30 P.M. 6 1/2

Friday 4 1 P.M.–10 P.M. Drawing & repairs 9

Third Panel

Saturday 5 10 a.m.–12 p.m. 14

Sunday 6 12 a.m.–7 p.m. Drawing 7

Monday 7 11:30 a.m.–9:30 p.m. 10

Sun 20 11 a.m.–8 a.m. (Mon) 21

Mon 21

29. E. P. Richardson interview by the author, 1978.

30. Lucienne Bloch interview by the author, 1986.

31. Wight n.d., box 1; see Rivera Mural Conservation Department files, DIA.

32. Lucienne Bloch interview by the author, January 1986.

33. Ernst Halberstadt interview by the author, January 1978.

34. Once Rivera arrived at the court he would continue to dawdle, smoking cigars with Halberstadt. "Rivera had one luxury. He would send me [Halberstadt] to the desk at the Wardell cigar counter with a dollar and a half. I could come back with three Garcia Grandes in glass tubes. . . . Best possible cigars. Imagine in 1932 what a fifty cent cigar was like. Probably like a ten dollar cigar today. And I would go to the newspaper stand and get three stogies for a nickel. They were sort of twisted and long. There are two kinds. There are the twisted Italian kind and the American Wheeling stogies which are like long lead pencils, about fifteen inches long. He would light up his cigar and I would light up a stogie. This went on every evening when he came to work, almost religiously he sent me out. He'd light up his Garcia Grande and I'd light up my stogie and we sat there puffing. One evening he said to me, 'What are you smoking?' I said, 'Here, try one of my stogies, and he said, 'Have one of my cigars.' For the next six months that was the routine. I'd come in and before I'd give him his cigars, I'd hand him one of my stogies and he said, 'Take one of mine.' So he sat there for a half hour smoking my two cent stogie and I smoked the Garcia Grande." Halberstadt in Detroit 1978a.

35. Spratling 1930, 164–166. All the assistants interviewed agreed that Rivera worked harder and longer than anyone else on the project. He rarely took days off. Dimitroff remembered the assistants kidding Rivera about his stamina: "Rivera had painted in the neighborhood of five hundred frescoes in Mexico. We counted them once for the sheer fun of it. . . . We had a joke, that Rivera has a new job. He is going to paint the pavement from Laredo, Texas, to Mexico City next." Dimitroff in Detroit 1978a.

36. Dimitroff in Detroit, 1978a.

37. Herrera 1983, 149.

38. Bloch 1932–1933.

39. Rivera 1991, 123–124.

40. Herrera 1983, 135.

41. Ibid.

42. "Edsel came to look at the murals three or four times a week. He was dressed casually." Halberstadt interview by the author, 1978.

Edsel Ford's 1932 appointment calendar reads: "Wed. June 22, 1932: Diego Rivera 9 AM Art Museum; Friday June 24, 1932: Rivera 10 AM Art Museum; Monday, June 27, 1932: Rivera 10:30; Thursday, October 27, 1932: Diego Rivera 9 A.M. Art Museum." Edsel Ford Papers, Ford Archives, Henry Ford Museum, box 306.

43. This studio is probably the secret one that Edsel hid from his father Henry on the fifth floor of the Briggs Plant in Detroit. At the time, Henry Ford and his factory managers believed that design was frivolous. See Tjaarda 1954.

44. Lucienne Bloch interview by the author, 1985. However, in June 1932, he spoke in French to an audience of two hundred women at the Belle Isle Casino with Lucienne Bloch as interpreter. They were members of the local committee on cultural relations with Latin America. The event was cosponsored by the International Institute of the YWCA. Rivera used the opportunity to speak of the need for peasant land reform in Mexico and to attack the conservative repressive direction of the former President Calles (who continued to maintain power during the presidencies of Emilio Portes Gil, Ortiz Rubio, and Abelardo Rodríguez). Bloch 1932–1933 and *The Detroit News*, June 3, 1932.

45. Sterne 1973, 109; for information on deported Mexicans see: Guerin-Gonzales 1994, 103. A group of transported Mexicans and Mexican American citizens from Detroit were settled at Hacienda El Coloso near Acapulco in December 1933.

46. Delpar 1992, 82.

47. Bloch 1932–1933, March 1933.

48. Edsel Ford Papers File #6, Ford Archives, Henry Ford Museum, box 316.

49. Ernst Halberstadt interview by the author, January 1978.

Chapter Three

1. Paul Cret was born in Lyons, France, and studied at the Ecole des Beaux-Arts in Paris. In 1903 he moved to the United States to teach architecture at the University of Pennsylvania. Beaux-Arts architecture is characterized by symmetrical plans that are based on the study of ancient monumental architecture. For Cret's "embittered" reaction to Rivera's transformation of the Court, see Marnham 1998, 245.

2. Grossman 1980, 99.

3. Ibid., 103.

4. Wolfe 1963, 304.

5. O'Connor in Detroit 1986, 215.

6. Davies 1933.

7. Rivera 1933, 289–295.

8. For a discussion of Fordism, see Allen 1996, 280–304.

9. Rivera 1933, 289.

10. Ibid., 291.

11. Ibid., 289.

12. Ibid.

13. Wm. H. Beatty, "All Around Detroit," *Daily News*, May 1, 1932, Ford Motor Company Scrapbook #80, Ford Archives: "Largest commercial transport plane now completed at Ford airport. Rivera will probably want to see it." The Ford Tri-Motor was adapted from the Fokker, a single-engine plane that formed the basis of air cargo transport in 1932. (See *Aviation*, November 1932, researched by Benjamin Sweetwine.)

14. Rivera 1933, 291.

15. Davies 1933.

16. Ibid.

17. Bloch 1932–1933.

18. Allen 1996, 285.

19. Davies 1933.

20. Ibid.

21. Rodriguez 1986, 42.

22. Moyssén 1977, 58; Wolfe 1963, 307.

23. Rodriguez 1986, 21.

24. *Ford Mines and Mineral Operations*. Ford Motor Co. booklet, 1978, Ford Archives, Dearborn, Michigan.

25. Davies 1933.

26. Rosa Casanova in Acevedo 1984, 119–129.

27. Ibid.

28. Rodriguez 1986, 43.

29. Ibid.

30. Ibid.

31. Ibid.

32. The Ford Motor Company had coal and gas properties in Kentucky, one of the richest coal producing areas in the United States.

33. McMeekin 1986, 45.

34. Davies 1933.

35. Wolfe 1963, 307.

36. McMeekin 1986, 50.

37. Binder 1995, 12.

38. Davies 1933.

39. McMeekin 1986, 26.

40. E. P. Richardson interview by the author, 1978, DIA Museum Archives.

41. McMeekin 1986, 32; see diagrams on 31, 33.

42. Ibid.

43. Sterne 1973, 109.

44. Rivera, Diego. *Interview* [Typewritten transcript translated by Lenore de Martinez, 1978] Caedmon record, 1950.

45. In the early 1950s, when Fritsch was retiring, Parke-Davis requested a photograph of the fresco portrait with the intention of presenting it to him as a parting gift. When the retirement party planners received the photograph, however, they declined to use it, saying that it was most unflattering. E. P. Richardson recalled that this was the only negative response to any of the portraits in the murals. Richardson interview by the author, 1978.

46. Wolfe 1963, 311; Moyssén 1977, 55; and Kozloff 1973, 62.

47. McMeekin 1986, 52.

48. Ibid., 37.

49. Wolfe 1963, 308.

50. Letter to the author from Dow chemical engineers, 1980.

51. The *Burning of Judas* fresco panel at the Secretaría de Educación Pública is an early example. The only other major painting that incorporates futuristic movement of the human figure is *Homage to Ana Merida* (1952), which captures the famous Mexican dancer's explosive arabesques in a variety of modern and folk dance movements and costumes.

52. Charles Darwin in *On the Origin of Species* (1859) quoted in McMeekin 1986, 46.

53. E. P. Richardson interview by the author 1978, DIA Museum Archives.

54. Ferry 1987, 52.

55. Dabrowski 1998, 307.

56. Wilson 1933, 230. In the February 1933 issue of *Fortune* magazine the Detroit murals were reproduced, accompanied by an article on the sugar business, which appears as a two-page spread. On the left are photographs of two workers in a sugar beet field titled "The Soil and Its Servants." On the right page are the presidents, identified by name, of various sugar companies and an image of sugar beet processing machines titled, "The Machines and their Masters." This parallels the dichotomy of anonymous workers and identified capitalists as is seen in the Detroit murals. The captions under each worker's photograph read "Spanish-American," "Mexican-Indian," "Russo-German," and "Sino-Japanese." The workers are defined by their race and the capitalists are defined by their names and titles. Rivera defines the worker in political terms, as a communist on the left wall, and he gave specific identities to the industrialists. "The Greenhouse Farm Flower," *Fortune*, February 1933, 7, no. 2, 56–57.

57. Identified by Robert Danto, who lived next door to Bricker.

Chapter Four

1. Braun 1993, 192.

2. Valentiner is quoted by Wight as saying that Rivera had only used one out-of-date machine. He was referring to the stamping press on the south wall automotive panel. The sketches (Wight n.d.) Rivera made at the Rouge indicate that he had actually seen more modern models. The presses had been sheathed to cover the interior mechanisms. The stamping press in the south wall automotive panel has the interior mechanisms exposed and is exactly the same as the 1927 model that Sheeler transformed into an image of power in his photograph of that year. Rivera could have seen the 1927 stamping presses in operation at the Rouge, but no sketch appears of this earlier model. It is more likely that Rivera saw it in photographic form, either Sheeler's single image, which had been published in *Ford News* in 1929, or the enlarged and halved version of the same photograph that formed part of the triptych that appeared in the Museum of Modern Art exhibition "Murals by American Painters and Photographers," from May 3–31, 1932.

3. Lavin 1990.

4. Lang and Williams, 375.

5. Ibid.

6. Wood 1993, pp. 253–254

7. Smith 1993.

8. Oles and Ferragut 1993, 10.

9. Azuela 1983.

10. Rivera 1933, 293.

Chapter Five

1. Franklin M. Peck, "Rivera Was a Jolly Lad," with lyrics to the tune of "Columbo." Printed broadside, Clyde Burroughs file 10, DIA Museum Archives.

The remaining verses read:

Ten months he studied, sketched, and drew,
In person and by proxy;
He sketched machines and furnaces
And playful streptococci.
And as he worked his spirit grew—
The city was a tonic—
His fertile pencil ranged from Fords
To babies embry-on-ic.

Oh, jolly old Diego,
His nudes were fat and round-o,
That communistic, capitalistic,
Son-of-a-gun Diego!

He sketched exactly what he saw,
The curators inform us . . .
He painted ladies up above,
With mammaries enormous.

But if he sketched just what he saw,
There's one thing sure does beat us,
I think it very marvelous
That he should sketch a fetus!

Oh, jolly old Diego,
His nudes were fat and round-o,
That photographic, pornographic,
Son-of-a-gun Diego!

He painted mass production and
He painted poison gases,
He painted aviators and
The well-known lower classes.

He did a woman on the east,
With a large and bulging form,
And if you slept a night with her,
You'd certainly be warm.

He did another woman, too,
I think her name was Myrtle,
With apples cradled in her arm
To show that she was fertile!

Oh, jolly old Diego,
His nudes were fat and round-o,
That clergy baitin', irritatin'
Son-of-a-gun Diego!

At last the job was finished and
The people flocked inside,
The clergy took one hasty look
And they were horrified!

They pointed shaking fingers at
The panel of diseases,
And said the vaccinated child
Was no one else but Jesus!

Oh, jolly old Diego,
His enemies abound-o
That most prodigious, sacrilegious,
Son-of-a-gun Diego!

About the meaning of the work
There grew an awful schism,
Some people called the frescoes art,
Some called 'em communism,

They said: "If you had shown our soul
We wouldn't so much mind it,"
Rivera said; "I looked for it,
But gosh, I couldn't find it!"

Oh, jolly old Diego,
His nudes were fat and round-o,
Materialistic, somewhat fistic
Son-of-a-gun Diego!

The clergy said the white capped nurse
Was Mary, Jesus's Mummy,
And folks who figure otherwise
Were dumber than a dummy!

Which shows how keen the clergy are
When they get down to clergin'
A single glance and they could tell
That nursie was a Virgin!

Oh, jolly old Diego,
He lost a lot of pound-o,
That very eleemosynary
Son-of-a-gun Diego!

The white-haired ladies came and shrieked
And went to seek ablution,
Because the frescoes had no Daugh-
Ters of the Revolution.

And when Diego left the town,
He must have thought it funny,
That after eighteen months of work,
He didn't get his money!

Oh, jolly old Diego,
Where did your promised pay-go,
You very learned, unconcerned
Son-of-a-gun Diego!

2. Brenner 1953. Anita Brenner was born Leah Brenner in Mexico; grew up in Texas; and studied literature in Mexico, earning a Ph.D. from the Universidad Nacional Autónoma de Mexico. She acted as Rivera's secretary during her student years and later published books and articles on Mexico in the United States. (See Glusker 1998.)

3. *The Detroit Collegian*, October 20, 1932; December 15, 1932; February 27, 1933; March 24, 1933; March 28, 1933; March 29, 1933; April 5, 1933.

4. Nicholson 1987, 26.

5. Valentiner files, DIA Museum Archives.

6. For a listing of all newspaper articles and correspondence related to the controversy, see Azuela 1986.

7. *Detroit Free Press*, March 21, 1933.

8. *Evening Times*, March 21, 1933.

9. Wolfe 1963, 312.

10. Valentiner's call for help was met with many telegrams and letters supporting the murals. Among supportive museum directors were Holger Cahill, director of the Museum of Modern Art; Jere Abbott, director of the Smith College Museum of Art; Robert Harshe, director of the Art Institute of Chicago; and Francis Henry Taylor, director of the Worcester Art Museum. Bryson Burroughs, the painting curator of the Metropolitan Museum of Art in New York, wrote in support and added that the Metropolitan had a Rivera fresco fragment on view that the artist had given to Mr. Dwight Morrow (March 25, 1933, DIA Museum Archives).

Artists such as Rockwell Kent wrote to Valentiner. Art organizations such as the College Art Association and the San Francisco Artists Association and instructors of art from the Dayton Art Museum sent letters of support, as did Frederick A. Blossom, editor of *Creative Art*. See Azuela 1986.

11. "Detroit Put on Art Map by Rivera, Asserts Kahn," *Detroit News*, March 22, 1933.

12. E. P. Richardson interview by the author 1978, DIA Museum Archives.

13. "Will Detroit, Like Mohammed II, Whitewash Its Rivera Murals?" *Art Digest* 7, April 1, 1933.

14. Ibid.

15. Valentiner files, DIA Museum Archives.

16. Ibid.

17. "Rivera Murals Are Accepted, *Detroit News*, April 12, 1933.

18. Wolfe 1963, 314.

19. Helm 1941, 54.

20. Fred L. Black Memoirs, Ford Archives, Henry Ford Museum, Dearborn, Michigan.

21. Ibid.

22. Ibid.

23. Ibid.

24. Ibid.

25. People's Museum Association, Articles of Incorporation, DIA Museum Archives.

26. Ibid.

27. E. P. Richardson interview by the author, 1978.

28. See Journal of the City Council 1933, Detroit, Michigan.

29. Wight n.d.

Epilogue

1. Hurlburt 1989, 172.

2. Detroit 1986, 109.

3. Wolfe 1963, 389.

4. In 1937 Rivera and Kahlo provided a safe haven in Mexico for the Bolshevik revolutionary Leon Trotsky. Rivera was severely criticized by the Mexican Communist Party for his support of Stalin's enemy. He made several unsuccessful attempts to be readmitted to the Communist Party and gained ground when he painted the 1952 painting for the Bellas Artes. However, it was not until immediately after Kahlo's death in 1954 that he was officially readmitted.

5. Wolfe 1963, 389.

6. *A Statement for the public by the Director, E. P. Richardson March, 1952.*

Detroit and Its Significance Painted by Diego Rivera, July 25, 1932 to March 13, 1933. . . Rivera was invited here by the Arts Commission in 1932 to decorate this room because he was considered the outstanding mural painter of our time. He came fresh from his first great series of murals in Mexico on which his world fame had been built. He was given no directions but asked simply to paint something related to Detroit. He chose to paint Detroit's mass production industry and technology. Coming from a handcraft civilization, he saw Detroit's industrial power with the eyes of an intelligent outsider for whom American industrial power and the enormous production made possible by our combination of scientific knowledge and engineering, were wholly new experiences. He saw a gigantic new force transforming twentieth-century life and that Detroit was its focal point. He chose, therefore, to paint its typical manifestation—the making of an automobile— as his main theme. . . . The panel which has aroused most controversy is that of Preventive Medicine. Rivera's idea here was to show in the doctor, the nurse and the child being vaccinated, the ancient symbolism of the man and woman and the child as the hope of the future. In the background, scientists in their library are a type of wise men searching for knowledge for the benefit of mankind. In the foreground are the animals which were once used for burnt sacrifices, now used for serum to defend humanity against diseases. The panel was painted with a serious intention of showing the nobility of science in its beneficent aspect. Rivera has painted on other occasions with deliberate intent to annoy. In this case, he had no such intention and the controversy which is centered about this panel was entirely unforeseen. As you look around you will see how the two-edged nature of our modern science haunted Rivera. It turns up in the two sides of the panel Flight and in the two panels of flying birds, as well as in the panels of Preventive Medicine and Poison Gas.

7. Report Of The Arts Commission To The Common Council: *We have received the copy of the resolution submitted by Councilman Eugene I. Van Antwerp together with your request for a report on the Rivera murals. We regret that Rivera's present behavior has revived the old controversy about the frescoes. There is no question that Rivera enjoys making trouble and loves being the center of a controversy. It is also a natural tendency to confuse the man and his work. But this man, who often behaves like a spoiled child, is also one of the outstanding talents of the western hemisphere. We believe in the Detroit frescoes we have one of the best as well as one of the most serious of his works. There is no other artist in the world today who could have painted murals of such magnitude and such force. They have become, in their twenty years of existence, world famous as examples of modern mural painting.*

When the frescoes were first executed, the novelty of their style shocked many people. Their elaborate symbolism seemed at first puzzling and confusing. But we believe the resentment against the Detroit murals has been caused by what Rivera has done elsewhere, not by what he did here.

The common objections to these murals have been (1) To Rivera's personal character, his style of art, his nationality—in short, to Rivera. This is an objection we can do little about. (2) That there is communistic propaganda in the murals. This we cannot discover. It seems to be only a misreading of his work, based upon his reputation, rather than on what appeared in these pictures. (3) That the Detroit workmen represented are ugly, therefore Rivera was insulting them. Would there have been any gain in truthfulness if Rivera had made them look conventionally handsome? All but one of these are portraits. Some of our museum guards posed for certain of the figures and have never taken offense at their portraits. (4) That they are blasphemous. This charge has been leveled at the panel of Preventive Medicine which, to be understood, must be considered with the companion panel of the Manufacture of Poison Gas. Rivera here was talking about the two-edged nature of modern science, something which has been driven home to all of us by the atomic bomb. Rivera is only exceptional in talking about this in painting rather than words.

Science and its applications have given us wonderful drugs, better health, better transportation, better communications, greater comforts: it has also given us terrible powers of destruction and cruelty. Rivera painted this as one of the important facts behind our technology. He has made the men who are preparing Poison Gas look, in dehumanized masks, like a modern echo of the demons from hell carved on the Medieval cathedrals. He has made the beneficent figures of healing science a modern echo of the divine in human life.

Is this irreverence? We believe that it is not irreverent but rather a striking piece of imagery which, especially as coming from an unbeliever, is a tribute to Christianity's meaning for the minds of men.

That they are decadent. We find nothing to support this. We find instead that Rivera is attacked because of resentment at various things he has done in his long career in Mexico. These murals of Detroit were intended, however, as a tribute to Detroit's industry and power of production, of which we are all proud. They have been widely recognized as works of great artistic brilliance and power. In our opinion, we should keep the frescoes as important works of modern art. The best answer which the City of Detroit can give to Rivera's present pro-Soviet propaganda efforts is to ignore them.

Dated April 1952. E. P. Richardson files, DIA Museum Archives.

8. Interview with E. P. Richardson by the author, 1978. DIA Museum Archives.

9. Cummings accurately characterized the group concerned about the stairwell design in a memo to the Arts Commission:

The audience concerned involves the younger group of preservationists on the staff and in the community plus the old-time Detroiters who feel the Rivera murals are the essential expression of Detroit's cultural life. A few union representatives have expressed concern but this is not a fight by the union for an essential expression of Detroit's workers. The art historians who have expressed concern are thus far limited in number, and on the whole this expression seems artificial, as opposed to the very real nostalgia and emotional devotion to the museum as expressed by long-time Detroiters.

Frederick J. Cummings to the Arts Commission, October 24, 1979; DIA Museum Archives.

10. Letter from J. Carter Brown to Frederick J. Cummings, December 21, 1979, DIA Museum Archives.

11. Sterne 1973, 94.

12. O'Connor 1978; Silk 1980; Kozloff 1973.

13. Smith 1993, 205.

14. Craven 1997, 134.

15. Kozloff 1973, 60.

16. Billeter and Bechler 1987, 55

BIBLIOGRAPHY

Acevedo 1984
Acevedo, Esther, et al. *Guía de murales del centro histórico de la Ciudad de Mexico.* Mexico City: Consejo Nacional de Fomento Educativo, 1984.

Allen 1996
Allen, John, "Fordism and Modern Industry." In Hall, Stuart, et al., eds. *Modernity: An Introduction to Modern Societies.* Cambridge, Massachusetts: Blackwell Publishers, 1996, pp. 280–304.

Alpern 1986
Alpern, Ron. *Rivera's Labor Legacy: The Detroit Murals,* Detroit Labor History Tours, 1986. Audiocasette.

Alpern 1989
———. *Detroit's Labor Legacy: The Detroit Murals* (history of unions and interviews with Ford workers). 26 minutes. Detroit Labor History Tours, 1989. Videocassette.

Azuela 1983
Azuela, Alicia. "Diego Rivera in Detroit: A Change of Ideology." Symposium paper for the 50th Anniversary of the Diego Rivera Murals in Detroit, the Detroit Institute of Arts, March 1983.

Azuela 1985
———. *Diego Rivera en Detroit.* Mexico City: Universidad Nacional Autónoma de Mexico, Instituto de Investegaciones Estéticas, 1985.

Babson et al. 1986
Babson, Steve, with Ron Alpern, Dave Elsila, and John Revitte. *Working Detroit: The Making of a Union Town.* Detroit: Wayne State University Press, 1986.

Bell 1980
Bell, Michael. Letter to the author recording interviews with two retired Dow Chemical employees, December 11, 1980.

Billeter and Bechler 1987
Billeter, Erika, and Marianne Bechler, eds. *Images of Mexico.* Federal Republic of Germany: Schirn Kunsthalle Frankfurt, 1987.

Binder 1995
Binder, Dr. Timothy A. *In the Wave Lies the Secret of Creation.* Waynesboro, Va.: University of Science and Philosophy, Swannanoa, 1995.

Bloch 1932–1933
Bloch, Lucienne. Diaries. 1932–1933.

Bloch and Dimitroff 1979–1989
Bloch, Lucienne, and Stephen Dimitroff. Correspondence with the author, Museum Archives, The Detroit Institute of Arts, 1979–1989.

Braun 1993
Braun, Barbara. *Pre-Columbian Art and the Post-Columbian World: Ancient American Sources of Modern Art.* New York: Harry N. Abrams, Inc., 1993.

Brenner 1953
Brenner, Anita. "Summer in Mexico," *Art News* 52, no. 54, Summer 1953, p. 55.

Camerini 1986
Camerini, Michael. *Diego Rivera's Frescoes* (comprehensive presentation of all major murals by Rivera, includes documentary film footage of Rivera painting). 60 minutes. The Detroit Institute of Arts, 1986. 35 mm film and videocassette.

Catlin 1966
Catlin, Stanton Loomis. *Art of Latin America since Independence.* New Haven and Austin: The Yale University Art Gallery and the University of Texas Art Museum, 1966.

Cervantes 1978
Cervantes, Maria Antonieta. *Treasures of Ancient Mexico from the National Anthropological Museum.* New York and Geocolor, S.A., Barcelona: Crescent Books, 1978.

Charlot 1979
Charlot, Jean. *The Mexican Mural Renaissance, 1920–1925.* New York: Hacker Art Books, 1979.

Cleveland 1999
Diego Rivera: Art & Revolution. The Cleveland Museum of Art & Mexico City: Instituto Nacional de Bellas Artes, 1999.

Craven 1997
Craven, David. *Diego Rivera as Epic Modernist.* New York: G.K. Hall & Co., 1997.

Cruden 1932
Cruden, Robert L. "Open Letter to Edsel Ford, *New Masses,* 7, no. 10, April 1932, p. 23.

Dabrowski 1998
Dabrowski, Magdalena; Dickerman, Leah; Galassi, Peter. *Aleksandr Rodchenko.* New York: The Museum of Modern Art, 1998.

Davies 1933
Davies, Florence. "Rivera Tells Meaning of Art Institute Murals," *The Detroit News,* January 19, 1933, p. 4.

Delpar 1992
Delpar, Helen. *The Enormous Vogue of Things Mexican: Cultural Relations Between the United States and Mexico, 1920–1935.* Tuscaloosa and London: University of Alabama Press, 1992.

Detroit 1978
The Detroit Institute of Arts. *The Rouge: The Image of Industry in the Art of Charles Sheeler and Diego Rivera.* Essays by Linda Downs and Mary Jane Jacob, 1978.

Detroit 1978a
Transcript of panel discussion held September 20, 1978, at the Detroit Institute of Arts. Museum Archives, DIA.

Detroit 1983
Transcript of panel discussion held March 20, 1978, at the Detroit Institute of Arts.

Detroit 1986
Diego Rivera: A Retrospective. The Detroit Institute of Arts and New York: W. W. Norton, 1986.

Dimitroff 1986
Dimitroff, Stephen Pope. *Apprentice to Diego Rivera and Fresco Workshops Manual.* Copyright Stephen Pope Dimitroff, 1986.

Downs 1979
Downs, Linda. "Diego Rivera's Portrait of Edsel Ford," *Bulletin of the DIA* 57, no. 1, 1979, pp. 47–52.

Ferry 1987
Ferry, W. Hawkins. *The Legacy of Albert Kahn.* Detroit: Wayne State University Press, 1987 (first published by the Detroit Institute of Arts, 1970).

Flores 1934
Flores, Andres Sanchez. "The Technique of Fresco," *The Architectural Forum* 60, no. 1, January 1934, pp. 7–16.

Ford 1920–1943
The Personal Records Resulting from the Activities of the Office of Edsel B. Ford, President of the Ford Motor Company, 1920–1943. Dearborn, Michigan: Ford Motor Company Archives. Edsel B. Ford Office, Accession 6.

Freedland 1987
Freedland, Sheryl. "Diego Rivera in Detroit: A City Raises Its Voice." Senior thesis, Detroit: Wayne State University, 1987.

Glusker 1998
Glusker, Susannah Joel. *Anita Brenner: A Mind of Her Own.* Austin: University of Texas, 1998

Grossman 1980
Grossman, Elizabeth Greenwell. "Paul Philippe Cret: Rationalism and Imagery in American Architecture." Ph.D. dissertation, Providence, R.I.: Brown University, June 1980, p. 99.

Grossman 1996
———. *The Civic Architecture of Paul Cret.* New York: Cambridge University Press, 1996.

Guerin-Gonzales 1994
Guerin-Gonzales, Camille. *Mexican Workers and American Dreams: Immigration, Repatriation, and California Farm Labor, 1900–1939.* New Brunswick, New Jersey: Rutgers University Press, 1994.

Helm 1941
Helm, MacKinley. *Modern Mexican Painters*. New York: Harper and Brothers., Inc., 1941.

Herrera 1983
Herrera, Hayden. *Frida: A Biography of Frida Kahlo*. New York: Harper and Row, Publishers, Inc., 1983.

Hurlburt 1989
Hurlburt, Laurance P. *The Mexican Muralists in the United States*. Albuquerque: The University of New Mexico Press, 1989.

Kettenmann 1997
Ketterman, Andrea. *Diego Rivera: A Revolutionary Spirit in Modern Art*. Cologne: Taschen, 1997.

Kozloff 1973
Kozloff, Max. "The Rivera Frescoes of Modern Industry and The Detroit Institute of Arts: Proletarian Art under Capitalist Patronage," *Artforum* 12, no. 3, November 1973, pp. 58–63.

Kurnitzky and Beck 1982
Kurnitzky, Horst, and Barbara Beck, eds. *Wand Bild Mexico*. Nationalgalerie Berlin, 1982.

Lang and Williams 1972
Lang, Berel, and Forrest Williams, eds. *Marxism and Art: Writings in Aesthetics and Criticism*. New York: David McKay Company, Inc., 1972.

Lavin 1990
Lavin, Marilyn Aronberg. *The Place of Narrative: Mural Decoration in Italian Churches, 431–1600*. Chicago and London: The University of Chicago Press, 1990.

Marnham 1998
Marnham, Patrick. *Dreaming With His Eyes Open: The Life of Diego Rivera*. New York: Alfred A. Knopf, 1998

McMeekin 1986
McMeekin, Dorothy. *Diego Rivera: Science and Creativity in the Detroit Murals*. East Lansing: Michigan State University Press, 1986.

Mexico City 1951
Diego Rivera: 50 Años de su Labor Artistica, Exposicion de Homenaje Nacional. Mexico City: Museo Nacional de Artes Plásticas, Departamento de Artes Plásticas, Instituto Nacional de Bellas Artes, 1949 (catalogue published 1951).

Moyssén 1977
Moyssén, Xavier. "El Retrato de Detroit por Digeo Rivera," *Anales del Instituto de Investigaciones Estéticas* 13, no. 47, 1977.

Nevins and Hill 1933
Nevins, Allan, and Frank Ernest Hill. *Ford: Expansion and Challenge, 1915–1933*. New York: Charles Scribner's Sons, 1933.

Newhouse 1978
Newhouse, Shelby. *The Age of Steel*, (focus on *Detroit Industry* frescoes with documentary film footage of Rivera painting). 60 minutes. The Detroit Institute of Arts, 1978. 35 mm film and videocassette.

New York 1992
The Great Utopia: The Russian and Soviet Avant-Garde, 1915–1932. New York: Solomon R. Guggenheim Museum, 1992.

The New York Times 1933
"Diego Rivera: A Crusader of Art," *New York Times Magazine*, April 2, 1933.

Nicholson 1987
Nicholson, Erick. "Diego Rivera and the Modern Aesthetic." Research paper, Ann Arbor: University of Michigan, May 15, 1987.

O'Connor 1977
O'Connor, Francis V. "The Diego Rivera Murals." Lecture presented at the Detroit Institute of Arts, March 20, 1977. Photocopy.

Oles 1993
Oles, James. *South of the Border: Mexico in the American Imagination, 1914–1947*. Translated by Marta Ferragut. Washington and London: Smithsonian Institution Press, 1993.

Paine 1931
Paine, Frances Flynn. *Diego Rivera*. New York: The Museum of Modern Art, December 23–January 27, 1931–32.

Pierrot and Richardson 1933
Pierrot, George F., and, Edgar P. Richardson. *The Diego Rivera Frescoes: A Guide to the Murals of the Garden Court*. Detroit: People's Museum Association, 1933. Republished as *An Illustrated Guide to the Diego Rivera Frescoes*. The Detroit Institute of Arts, 1934.

Quirarte 1982
Quirarte, Jacinto. "The Coatlicue in Modern Mexican Painting," *Research Center for the Arts Review* 5, no. 2, April 1982, p. 5.

Rivera 1933
Rivera, Diego. "Dynamic Detroit—An Interpretation," *Creative Art*, 12, no. 4, April 1933, pp. 289–295.

Rivera 1933a
Rivera, Diego. "What Is Art For?" *The Modern Monthly* 8, June 1933, pp. 275–278.

Rivera 1934
Rivera, Diego. "Diego Rivera on Architecture and Mural Painting," *The Architectural Forum* 60, no. 1, January 1934, pp. 3–6.

Rivera [1950?]
Rivera, Diego. "Interview." Caedmon Recording. Transcript translated by Lenore de Martinez, 1978.

Rivera 1978
Diego Rivera: The Age of Steel, dir. Shelby Newhouse, 30 min., Kultur, 1978. Videocassette.

Rivera 1986
Portrait of an Artist: The Frescoes of Diego Rivera, dir. Michael Camerini, 35 min., Home Vision, 1986. Videocassette.

Rivera 1989
Rivera's Labor Legacy: The Detroit Murals, dir. Ron Alpern, 26 min., Detroit Labor History Tours, 1989. Videocassette.

Rivera 1991
Rivera, Diego, with Gladys March. *My Art, My Life: An Autobiography*. New York: Dover Publications, Inc., 1991.

Rodríguez 1969
Rodríguez, Antonio. *A History of Mexican Mural Painting*. New York: Putnam, 1969.

Rodríguez 1986
Rodríguez, Antonio. *Canto a la tierra: Los Murales de Diego Rivera en la Capilla de Chapingo*. Carretera México—Texcoco: Universidad Autónoma Chapingo, 1986.

Rodríguez 1991
Rodríguez, Antonio. *Diego Rivera: Mural Painting*. Mexico City: Fondo Editorial de la Plástica Mexicana, Trusteeship in the Banco Nacional de Comercio Exterior, 1991.

San Francisco 1930
Diego Rivera. San Francisco: California Palace of the Legion of Honor, November 15–December 25, 1930.

Silk 1980
Silk, Gerald D. "The Image of the Automobile in American Art," *Michigan Quarterly Review*, Fall–Winter 1980.

Smith 1993
Smith, Terry. *Making the Modern: Industry, Art, and Design in America*. Chicago and London: The University of Chicago Press, 1993.

Spratling 1930
Spratling, William P. "Diego Rivera," *Mexican Folkways* 6, no. 4, 1930.

Sterne 1973
Sterne, Margaret. "The Museum Director and the Artist: Dr. William R. Valentiner and Diego Rivera in Detroit." In *Detroit in Perspective*, Winter 1973, pp. 88–110.

Sterne 1980
Sterne, Margaret. *The Passionate Eye: The Life of William R. Valentiner*. Detroit: Wayne State University Press, 1980.

Tjaarda 1954
Tjaarda, John. "Trends in Automotive History: How the Lincoln-Zephyr Was Born," *Motor Trend*, February 1954, pp. 30–33, 63.

Trotsky 1925
Trotsky, Leon. "Proletarian Culture and Proletarian Art," *Literature and Art*, 1925. In Lang and Williams 1972.

Werckmeister, 1998
Werckmeister, O.K. "Rivera, Rodin, Meunier and Marx: Skizze zu den Wandbildern in Detroit," *Zeitenspiegelung*, Berlin, 1998.

Wight n.d.
Wight, Clifford. Collected Papers. Syracuse University Library, Syracuse, New York, Boxes 1 and 2.

Wills 1937
Wills, Helen. *Fifteen-Thirty: The Story of a Tennis Player*. New York and London: Charles Scribner's Sons, 1937.

Wilson 1933
Wilson, Edmund. "Detroit Paradoxes," *The New Republic*, July 12, 1933, pp. 230–233.

Wolfe 1963
Wolfe, Bertram David. *The Fabulous Life of Diego Rivera*. New York: Stein and Day Publishers, 1963.

Wolfe n.d.
———. Papers, Hoover Archives, Stanford University.

Wood 1992
Wood, Paul. "The Politics of the Avant-Garde." In *The Great Utopia: The Russian and Soviet Avant-Garde, 1915–1932*. New York: Solomon R. Guggenheim Museum, 1992.

Wood 1993
Wood, Paul. "Realisms and Realities." In *Realism, Rationalism, Surrealism: Art Between the Wars*. New Haven: Yale University Press in Association with the Open University, 1993, pp. 251–253

PHOTO CREDITS

All color photography is from the Detroit Institute of Arts, unless otherwise noted.

All black and white photography was provided by the Museum Archives, the Detroit Institute of Arts, unless otherwise noted.

All 15.2 by 22.9 centimeter sketchbook drawings of 1932 are from the Rivera Archives, Mexico City.

Henry Ford Museum and Greenfield Village are located in Dearborn, Michigan.

Figure 8: *The Detroit News*

Figure 9: From the collections of Henry Ford Museum and Greenfield Village

Figure 10: Albert Kahn Architects, Detroit

Figure 11: Dirk Bakker

Figure 12: Rivera Archives

Figures 13 and 14: The *Detroit News*

Figures 16, 17, and 18: Rivera Archives

Figure 23: Clifford Wight Collection, Syracuse University Library

Figures 27 and 28: Rivera Archives

Figure 45: Museo Frida Kahlo

Figure 49: The Detroit Institute of Arts, Founders Society Purchase, Laura H. Murphy fund, 40.145

Figure 58: Museo Frida Kahlo

Figures 59 and 60: Collection of Dolores Olmedo

Figure 63: Clifford Wight Collection, Syracuse University Library

Figure 64: The Detroit Institute of Arts, Bequest of Eleanor Clay Ford, 77.5

Figure 65: The *Detroit News*

Figure 70: Rivera Archives

Figure 71: Rivera Archives

Figure 72: The Detroit Institute of Arts, Gift of the Artist, 33.39

Figure 74: Rivera Archives

Figure 75: The Detroit Institute of Arts, Gift of the Artist, 33.35

Figure 78: The Detroit Institute of Arts, Gift of the Artist, 33.43

Figure 80: The Detroit Institute of Arts, Gift of the Artist, 33.44

Figure 85: From the collections of Henry Ford Museum and Greenfield Village

Figure 87: Rivera Archives

Figure 88: Museum of Art, Rhode Island School of Design, Nancy Sales Day Fund, 68.026

Figure 89: Museo Nacional de Antropologia, Mexico City

Figure 92: From the collections of Henry Ford Museum and Greenfield Village

Figure 93: Rivera Archives

Figure 99: Rivera Archives

Figures 100 and 101: Leeds City Art Gallery, England

Figure 105: From the collections of Henry Ford Museum and Greenfield Village

Figure 106: Rivera Archives

Figure 111: The Detroit Institute of Arts, Gift of the Artist, 33.45

Figure 112: The Detroit Institute of Arts, Gift of the Artist, 33.47

Figure 113: Rivera Archives

Figure 114: The Detroit Institute of Arts, Gift of the Artist, 33.40

Figure 115: The Detroit Institute of Arts, Gift of the Artist, 33.42

Figure 118: The Detroit Institute of Arts, Gift of the Artist, 33.36

Figure 121: The Detroit Institute of Arts, Gift of the Artist, 33.41

Figure 124: North Carolina Museum of Art, Bequest of William Valentiner, G.65.10.550

Figure 127: Rivera Archives

Figure 128: The Detroit Institute of Arts, Gift of the Artist, 33.37

Figure 129: National Gallery of Art, Rosenwald Collection, Washington, D.C.

Figure 130: Philip J. and Suzanne Schiller Collection

Figure 124: The Detroit Institute of Arts, Gift of the Artist, 33.46

Figure 152: From the collections of Henry Ford Museum and Greenfield Village

Figure 154: From the collections of Henry Ford Museum and Greenfield Village

Figures 176 and 177: Rivera Archives

Figure 178: Leeds City Art Galleries, England

Figure 180: From Martin Friedman, *Charles Sheeler*, New York, 1975

Figure 181: From the collections of Henry Ford Museum and Greenfield Village

Figure 185: Museo Nacional de Antropologia, Mexico City

Figure 196: From the collections of Henry Ford Museum and Greenfield Village

Figure 208: Leeds City Art Gallery, England

Figure 236: Rivera Archives

Page numbers in *italics* refer to illustrations.